MW00773501

Advance Praise for *Young Zionist Voices*

"Reading this book is like taking all these brilliant young people out for coffee—and then listening, in silent awe, as they articulate their visions for the future. In a time of horror, here's some fantastic news: The Jewish future is in good hands."

— Dara Horn, author of *People Love Dead Jews*

"Throughout Jewish history, crisis has often summoned our finest qualities. As the assault on the legitimacy of the Jewish story grows, many of us have worried about the Jewish future. But as this essential collection of thoughtful and inspiring essays reveals, our future leadership is already emerging. This book is a gift of hope."

— Yossi Klein Halevi, senior fellow, Shalom Hartman Institute, author of the New York Times bestseller *Letters to My Palestinian Neighbor*

"In the shadow of Jewish catastrophe and turmoil, Young Zionist Voices offers the energy and vision of a new generation ready to shape the narrative, challenge the status quo, and take on the challenges of our time. These essays are not just ideas; they are the seeds of a vibrant, unbreakable Jewish future."

— Noa Tishby, co-author of the *New York Times* bestseller *Uncomfortable Conversations with a Jew*

"David Ben-Gurion, who went on to become Israel's first prime minister, started as a young, impassioned, Zionist Jew in the Diaspora. Within these essays hide the next Ben-Gurion, the next Golda Meir, the next Vladimir Jabotinsky and Rabbi Kook and Ahad Ha'am and Yitzhak Rabin and Abba Eban and Chaim Weizmann—and so many other future leaders of a new, strong, and proud Zionist movement. Now is the time to listen to what they have to say, to amplify their words, and to work to make their vision a reality."

— Shai Davidai, assistant professor, Columbia Business School

"Many years ago I argued that to a rising young generation of Jews, Zionism has become simply a shorthand for a confident Jewish identity. It therefore delights me immensely to witness a rising generation of young proud Jews, who are embracing their Jewish identity with the confidence spirit of Zionism, and that amidst these challenging times, are leaning into being Jewish, into the joy, into the history, into the future, and yes, into the fight. As with *Jewish Priorities*, David Hazony again has captured a moment, ushering a new cohort of Jewish voices that ensure that we will never lack for thinkers, writers and leaders."

– Einat Wilf, former MK, senior fellow, Z3 Institute, author of *We Should All Be Zionists*

"We graybeards, weary from years in the trenches defending Israel from its hateful detractors, often scoff at the next generation for being too glib, too soft, too aloof. How lucky are we, then, to thumb through Young Zionist Voices and find out that the kids are alright. From ruminations on theology to rousing calls to action, the contributions reflect a dizzying array of sensibilities and approaches. All, though, are thick with the one thing we could all use right now—hope. Anyone who still needs proof that Zionism is alive and kicking should pick up a copy and pass the baton with an easy heart."

– Liel Leibovitz, author of *How the Talmud Can Change Your Life* and co-host of Unorthodox Podcast

"Here are the voices—passionate, urgent, contradictory, clear—that will shape the Jewish future. They demand attention and they deserve respect. This anthology allows us to imagine what might be for our people in an uncertain and disorienting age."

– David J. Wolpe, Max Webb Emeritus Rabbi of Sinai Temple, Los Angeles, author of *Why Faith Matters*

"These young voices aren't just Zionist. They are calling for Jews to live committed, engaged lives advocating for our people wherever we find ourselves, with Israel as an anchor. May their message be heard by many who might otherwise be out of reach."

– Elisha Wiesel, Chairman, Elie Wiesel Foundation

Also by David Hazony

Jewish Priorities: Sixty-Five Proposals for the Future of Our People

The Ten Commandments: How Our Most Ancient Moral Text Can Renew Modern Life

New Essays on Zionism (with Yoram Hazony and Michael B. Oren)

Eliezer Berkovits: Essential Essays on Judaism

Eliezer Berkovits: God, Man, and History

Young Zionist Voices

A New Generation Speaks Out

Edited by David Hazony

Foreword by Eylon Levy

Afterword by Zack Bodner

A WICKED SON BOOK
An Imprint of Post Hill Press
ISBN: 979-8-88845-616-3
ISBN (eBook): 979-8-88845-617-0

Young Zionist Voices:
A New Generation Speaks Out
© 2024 by David Hazony
All Rights Reserved

Cover Design by Aura Lewis

Published in cooperation with the Z3 Project.
For more information visit Z3Project.org.

This book, as well as any other Wicked Son publications, may be purchased in bulk quantities at a special discounted rate. Contact orders@posthillpress.com for more information.

This is a work of nonfiction. All people, locations, events, and situations are portrayed to the best of the author's memory.

No part of this book may be reproduced, stored in a retrieval system, or transmitted by any means without the written permission of the author and publisher.

Post Hill Press
New York • Nashville
wickedsonbooks.com
posthillpress.com

Published in the United States of America
1 2 3 4 5 6 7 8 9 10

Contents

Foreword

Eylon Levy

On college campuses around the world, there is a new bully in the yard. The name-calling, threats, intimidation, and physical violence are not exactly new, but in the Campus Tentifada, the bullies have asserted their presence. Like antisemites throughout history, they are driven by a moral zeal, a conviction that excluding Jews is the noblest expression of virtue. From colleges to workplaces to city streets, the bullies feel they have the license to scare Jews, to shout them into submission. But there is one thing they did not take into account: You can pick on the Jews, but the Jews are no longer easy pickings.

The young writers, thinkers, and activists appearing in this collection are not simply Gen-Z. They are "Gen-Zionists": a new generation of Jews who understand this historical moment. Gen-Zionists stand up to bullies. They refuse

Eylon Levy is a former Israeli government spokesman, who represented Israel on international television and radio at the start of the October 7 War. He now heads the Israeli Citizen Spokespersons' Office and hosts the *State of a Nation* podcast and YouTube show. Eylon previously served as international media advisor to President Isaac Herzog, after a career as a television news anchor. He holds a B.A. in Philosophy, Politics, and Economics from the University of Oxford and an M.Phil. in International Relations from the University of Cambridge, and he served in the IDF after making Aliyah from the United Kingdom. He is the translator of several influential works of Hebrew non-fiction, including *Catch-67* by Micah Goodman and *The War of Return* by Einat Wilf and Adi Schwartz. He lives in Tel Aviv.

to be intimidated. They will not let anyone shame them for who they are. Around the world, young Jews are mobilizing to show antisemites that Jews fight back, Jews answer back, and Jews have each other's backs.

On October 7, 2023, young Israelis awoke to rocket sirens and discovered, to their horror, that the adults were not in the room. Nobody was coming to save them. Those who had weapons grabbed them to defend their fellow citizens; others mobilized to distribute aid to displaced families, setting up whole civilian kitchens and volunteering drives. They took responsibility. They took action.

Gen-Zionist is a generation of heroes, some of whom made the ultimate sacrifice. Heroes like 22-year-old Aner Shapira: When Hamas death squads threw grenades into a shelter where he and others were hiding at the Nova festival, he chucked seven back out, until the eighth took his life. Heroines like 26-year-old Liron Barda, the bartender who refused to evacuate from the scene of the music festival so that she could treat the wounded—and was murdered. They have shown fortitude that should shame many of their Western peers.

That same spirit of self-reliance is also being seen in the Diaspora, where young Jews increasingly have come to understand that if they do not stand up for themselves, nobody will stand up for them. That if their cousins in Israel have lost friends who fell in battle, they can certainly risk losing friends by falling out over politics. That if their cousins in Israel can face down Hamas in Gaza, they can face down Hamas fangirls on campus. That this is their moment.

* * *

October 7 triggered three momentous shifts in the Jewish world, setting the stage for the immense challenges that Gen-Zionists must confront in the years to come.

The first was the surprise rediscovery of a sense of collective purpose in Israel, after the ugliest period of political division in the nation's history. Suddenly, everyone realized that only one thing mattered: defending our homes and neighbors against a barbaric terrorist army. Nobody waited for orders. Everyone asked only what they could do to help. Israel witnessed a spontaneous civilian mobilization unlike anything the world had ever seen. A country that appeared to be tearing itself apart was suddenly unified as never before.

The second was the Great Diaspora Awakening, as Jews worldwide sprang into action to defend their Israeli brethren. They donated their jewelry, organized solidarity missions, volunteered, and sent planeloads full of gear for reservists. They opened their checkbooks, with the JFNA alone raising over $850 million for its Israel Emergency Fund. Rediscovering a sense of Jewish identity, they started wearing Magen Davids and plastering walls with hostage posters and anti-Hamas stickers. They also mobilized to push back against the pro-Hamas fever gripping their streets and elite institutions, determined to stare down a terrifying, self-righteous surge of antisemitism.

The third trend is still inchoate. It is the growing understanding that the fates of Israel and the Diaspora are inextricably intertwined. Neither can swim while the other sinks; neither can afford to ignore what is happening to the other. Diaspora Jews understand that if Israel is attacked, they too will not be allowed to live in peace. And Israelis understand that they cannot ignore the intellectual insanity unfolding across the "enlightened" world—and that the student radicals of today could be its allies' leaders of tomorrow. The Diaspora needs a strong Israel, and Israel needs a strong Diaspora. Jews must therefore make the world safe for Israel so that Israel can make the world safe for the Jews.

These positive trends, however, are not self-sustaining. They will require strong young Zionist voices to nurture and amplify them.

In February 2024, I flew from Tel Aviv to Atlanta to attend Hillel International's Israel Summit. Before my keynote speech, I spoke with the students to understand whether the situation on their campuses was really as bad as the reports I'd heard. "Who are your allies?" I asked them, and the reply was a room of blank stares. *Allies?* They felt abandoned, betrayed, and cast out.

They were facing classic schoolyard bully dynamics. The bullies were not the majority. But they were sufficiently numerous, loud, and violent to deter people from wanting to have anything to do with the kids who were getting picked on. Why put yourself on the bullies' blacklist? Far better to keep your head down, or even to join them.

At the gala event, I ditched my trademark blue-and-white suit for a specially printed t-shirt emblazoned with a victory sign and the slogan: "GEN-ZIONIST." The next day, I was mobbed as I handed out a thousand of the shirts, which many of the students then wore proudly as they checked in at Atlanta Airport. I soon started seeing pictures of Jewish students wearing them at campus counterprotests.

Gen-Zionist students are mobilizing to stand up to the bullies.

But they need support from the broader Jewish community. And they need leaders among them who will articulate their cause.

***

Exactly one month after October 7, David Hazony published an essay in *Sapir* Journal called "The War Against the Jews." Both timely and timeless, Hazony's *cri-de-coeur* will be remembered as one of the canonical texts of this turning point in Jewish history. In it, he makes the case that Hamas's invasion was the opening shot of a global war against the Jewish people. Jews everywhere, he warns, must now see themselves in a state of war against the rising "antisemitic hordes" and must prepare for battle accordingly. The essays in this collection are an important answer to Hazony's call.

"Stop acting like the benign ocean water that fuels the hurricane passing overhead," Hazony writes. "Instead, be the hurricane." Little could he have imagined that a song titled "Hurricane" would, months later, become one of the defining texts of this era, when Gen-Zionist heroine Eden Golan conquered Europe's biggest stage despite the braying mobs determined to silence her.

The voices in this collection *are* the hurricane.

"Every day I'm losing my mind," belted the 20-year-old singer at the Eurovision Song Contest in the notorious antisemitic stronghold of Malmö, Sweden, in May 2024. But the thirty-one young thinkers in this volume are putting their minds to work. And they are fortunate to do so under the editorial guidance of Hazony, who is a public intellectual in the finest sense: Through his leadership of the new Z3 Institute and his 2023 collection *Jewish Priorities*, he is working to resurrect the Jewish republic of letters for the so-called TikTok Generation.

The Gen-Zionists featured in this collection are thinking deeply about how to safeguard our eternal people in the latest stage of a forever war against them.

It bears repeating how strikingly countercultural this is. The majority of the contributors have gone through colleges that have brainwashed their peers with a simplistic, pseudointellectual view of the world that has left them receptive to daft, catchy slogans denying the validity of both the State of Israel and Jewish identity. These writers, however, have chosen to radically reevaluate the paradigms that have led us to this crisis.

They are not running headlong into battle. They realize that first, the Jewish people must perform some introspection, or what the Hebrew language so beautifully calls *heshbon nefesh*—an accounting of the soul. They understand that before we can strategize about solutions, we need to get our house in order and to offer a potent critique of the pre-October 7 era. Many of them feel, rightfully, that the Jewish establishment failed to evaluate the threat correctly. They have been let down, even betrayed, by the non-Zionist, anti-Zionist, or even only meekly-Zionist Jewish voices who thought they could achieve Jewish safety without fighting for the safety of the world's greatest Jewish collective, the State of Israel.

In *Young Zionist Voices*, you will find Gen-Zionists discussing not only how to stand up to bullies, but how to prepare their generation to stand up to them. They think about how to focus inward, before outward. About nurturing solidarity across our global family, including through authentic shared experiences between Diaspora and Israeli Jews; about "leaning in" to a renewed Jewish identity, both nourished by ancient traditions and deliberately broadened; about embracing our difference, both Jewish difference versus the rest of the world and difference within our ranks; and about cultivating pride in Israel and strengthening the bond between Judaism and Zionism, instead of trying to draw increasingly painful artificial distinctions.

It is no exaggeration to say that many of the contributors to *Young Zionist Voices* will shape the future of the Jewish people in the twenty-first century, in Israel and around the world. Their challenge is monumental, and they face it, as contributor Avi Gamulka puts it, as "the first generation to experience the world as consistently getting worse." Even before October 7, they were locked out of the housing ladder, their formative years had been upended by successive COVID lockdowns, mental health was in freefall, and global warming threatened to make the whole world inhospitable, if not uninhabitable.

But maybe, then, this is the reason that the Gen-Zionists are ready to inherit the mantle of Jewish leadership, or at least to demand an outsized voice at the table. They never had the luxury of thinking the world was going their way. Their generation has always known it would have to muster every fiber of creativity and entrepreneurship to reverse trends that the adults either denied, downplayed, or dismissed as inevitable. That primed them for this moment.

The Gen-Zionists have risen to the moment; the prospect of what they will yet achieve offers a powerful source of optimism, even inspiration, for the rest of us.

Introduction

David Hazony

The essays in this collection come from a new generation of Jewish thought leaders responding to the gravest crisis facing our people in more than half a century. Many of them will play key roles in Jewish life for decades to come. Others offer important insights that can help shape the new Jewish world that will emerge.

After October 7, Jews around the world faced a combination of fear, loneliness, and uncertainty about what to do—feelings that persist, in one form or another, to this day.

Younger Jews, and especially students, have carried the heaviest burden. They, after all, bore the brunt of the pro-Hamas protests that tore through elite universities beginning within hours of the assault. In a nightmarish echo of past traumas, Jewish students suddenly felt unwelcome, betrayed by friends and allies, and forced to declare their repudiation of Zionism or face social shunning or worse.

David Hazony is the Director and Steinhardt Senior Fellow at the Z3 Institute for Jewish Priorities. His anthology *Jewish Priorities: Sixty-Five Proposals for the Future of Our People* (Wicked Son, 2023) brings together writers from across the Jewish world to offer visions of the Jewish future. His book *The Ten Commandments: How Our Most Ancient Moral Text Can Renew Modern Life* (Scribner, 2010) was a finalist for the National Jewish Book Award. He previously edited two journals of Jewish and Israeli interest, as well as several volumes of Zionist and Jewish thought. He has a Ph.D. in Jewish Philosophy from the Hebrew University and lives in Jerusalem.

University presidents testifying before Congress made it clear that while America's top colleges promised protection to every other minority, Jews didn't count.

Yet it was also clear that some young people were looking for ways to fight back—with or without the support of established Jewish institutions. Spontaneously, it seemed, leaders emerged—on campuses, inside organizations, and in youth movements and communal institutions—determined to roll back the tide.

The aim of this book is to give this emerging young leadership a voice, through a collection of new essays pointing to a new future. The goal is to showcase a new generation of Jewish thought leaders pushing not only for bold on-the-ground activism but also for bold new thinking.

A significant number of the contributors are campus-based, while others have begun careers in Jewish life. Some come from Orthodox backgrounds, others secular, still others represent liberal Jewish movements. Most are based in the United States, but there are also Israelis, both native and recent *olim*, as well as writers from the United Kingdom, Australia, and Latin America. Their attitudes to religion, politics, and Jewish identity vary widely—but all of them are seeking to explain Zionism, and their role in it, in a new era.

What, after all, *is* Zionism after October 7? The urgency behind this question was borne out in a study conducted in the spring of 2024 by the Jewish Federations of North America. While 90 percent of American Jews agreed with the statement that "Israel has a right to exist as a Jewish state," only 46 percent expressly identified as Zionist. Five percent said they were anti-Zionist, 17 percent "non-Zionist," and a whopping 32 percent answered that they "don't know."

Clearly the word "Zionist" means many things to many people—including those who, like the contributors of this volume, accept the label on themselves. This book offers, among other things, a powerful battery of answers to that question, resting on foundations that range from religion to psychology to collective Jewish history.

* * *

Yet despite their disparate approaches and backgrounds, a few powerful themes emerge.

The most obvious one is that *fighting back is better than freezing up or fleeing.* Several of the essays focus on the nature of the response to Jew-hatred and what spiritual and communal energies inform that response. There is a sentiment that now is a time to fight, despite the understandable fears and generations of inculcated habits of conflict-avoidance. To be a Zionist, we learn from several of them, is to "lean in" to Jewish identity precisely where it is challenged, and to find the courage to defend it.

A second recurring theme is the *centrality of Israel to Jewish life today.* Perhaps it's predictable that a collection of Zionist essays will affirm the importance of Israel in young Jews' lives. But some go further—sharing their ineffable sense of belonging when visiting or living in the Jewish state, and also the belief that Israel's very existence alters their sense of what being Jewish is actually about. For some, it is no longer even possible to distinguish between "Judaism" and "Zionism."

Yet at the same time, there is in several of these essays an argument that *Zionism is about much more than Israel.* While generations of Diaspora Jews have identified Zionism with support for Israel and the "pro-Israel community," among the contributors there is a growing awareness that the word should mean something much deeper. As Einat Wilf has written in the 2023 essay collection *Jewish Priorities*, Zionism was never just about sovereignty or refuge; it was also, from the beginning, a kind of "therapeutic response" to antisemitism and the vulnerability of exile. In this new collection, contributors are calling for a more expanded view of Zionism—one that includes both strong Diaspora communities and the qualities of character that are just as important today as they were when Zionist writers started articulating them more than a century ago.

A fourth theme gets to the heart of Jewish identity in a post-October 7 world: that despite the crisis, *victimhood and fighting antisemitism cannot be the core of being Jewish.* These young leaders, at a moment of seemingly existential crisis, are looking beyond it. Standing tall as Jews, for many of them, requires first of all a redoubled investment in the positive historical, religious, and communal commitments to Jewish knowledge, practice, and peoplehood. Implicitly, there is a sharp critique of the strategies undertaken by established Jewish institutions over the last half century:

The enormous investments in Holocaust education and vast "defense organizations" have, for many of these writers, clearly missed the mark.

Finally, we see a desire to move beyond not only the long-established strategies of Jewish life, but beyond existing Jewish leadership as well. In its place, they argue, the time has come for *a new generation to lead the way*. This may be difficult for some readers to palate—especially philanthropists and Jewish professionals who have invested their lives in the existing Jewish structures. Yet their claim must be heard. After the failure of the older generations to identify the threat and prepare the next generation for the current challenges, these younger Jewish leaders and thinkers see themselves as better positioned and motivated to define the contours of Jewish life in the coming generation. It's time, they're saying, for the old guard to step aside.

* * *

In the pages that follow, you'll find this new generation calling for new ideas about everything being Jewish entails. Zionism for them is no longer just a political-activist position; it is a central pillar of the Jewish future. Some draw upon new readings of our collective past; others are deeply attuned to the prevailing winds of what is to come.

What they all share is not just an unflinching commitment to a flourishing Jewish people continuing far into the future, but also a creativity and dynamism that have been lacking in the Jewish discourse—an inner optimism that transcends the fear and pain which has, it seems, engulfed the conversations of older Jews.

You will not agree with every essay. Many contradict each other—as it should be. What you will find, however, is an energy, determination, and strength of spirit that can inspire us all in an especially hard moment in our history.

Hopefully, you'll also discover what I did when I first read these essays: that with thought leaders like these, the Jewish future is in far better hands than many have come to believe. In their light, it is hard to be a pessimist.

1

Youth Movements and the Power of the *Madrich*

Eli Akerman Himelfarb

I have been an active member of a Zionist youth movement, or *tnuat noar*, for almost my whole life. It was there that I learned most of what I know about Israel, Zionism and the Jewish people, and how to put the values they embody into practice. I had the opportunity to create and organize activities and events that very few people my age are able to do. It has been fundamental to who I am, and I believe it is an incredibly important part of the global Jewish future.

For this reason, I feel immensely privileged that I was able to become a *madrich*, or youth movement counselor. I have taken great inspiration from the role of the madrich through the years—and from the impressive achievements of *madrichim* and the role they played in building the Zionist movement and the Jewish state.

Born in Colombia, **Eli Akerman Himelfarb** is a lifelong *madrich* in Hanoar Hatzioni and studies International Relations and History at the Hebrew University of Jerusalem. He has studied Zionist history, Jewish identity, and Jewish-Zionist youth movements for over a decade, actively sharing his knowledge with future generations through informal education. Following a year studying International Relations in Colombia, he chose to serve as a combat soldier in the IDF.

Today, in the wake of October 7 and the immense challenge facing Jewish communities around the world, we need to give priority to every Zionist youth movement in the world, in order to form the next generations of Zionist educators, thinkers, and leaders. It is through the history of the youth movements that we encounter the essence of Zionism, which begins with the personal example of the madrichim and the unique qualities of character they embody.

* * *

Zionist youth movements began both under the inspiration of, and as a response to, the scouting movement that emerged in Europe and North America in the late nineteenth century—especially in Germany, the United Kingdom, and other European countries. Their objective was to give young boys and girls the tools they would need to gain prominence in society. They offered the image of a strong idealist who is connected to nature. According to Robert Baden-Powell, founder of the scouting movement in the United Kingdom and author of the 1908 manifesto *Scouting for Boys*, this meant learning different skills that would enable them to contribute to society in ways that were not common at the time. "Those who succeed best," he wrote, "are those who learnt scouting when they were still boys. Scouting also comes in very useful in any kind of life you take up, whether it is soldiering or even business life in a city." In 1910, the Boy Scouts of America was founded to teach boys "patriotism, courage, self-reliance, and kindred values."

This combination of outdoor skill-building, leadership, and character development spoke to many European Jews at the time—especially enlightened Jews who hoped to achieve true acceptance in Europe, but also Zionists who looked for a future when they would need many of the same qualities in building their own homeland.

Antisemitism was a serious problem, however. Even if some of the young Jews who wanted to join the scouts believed they had fully assimilated to European society, they were turned away. The scouting movement at that time, in Europe at least, was grounded in a race-based nationalism, and it simply had neither interest in, nor room for, Jews.

It was out of this refusal, combined with the rise of Zionism as a popular movement among many modern Jews, that Zionist scouting movements were born. Young Jews decided to challenge old notions and become masters of their own destiny. In the United States, Young Judaea was founded as the first American Zionist youth organization in 1909. In Europe, the first Jewish scout movement, Blau-Weiss (Blue-White), was launched in Germany in 1912. The name may sound Zionist, but this movement was at first unrelated to Zionism. It offered Jews similar values, methods, and education as did the general scouts. Joseph Markus from Breslau and Walter Moses from Berlin, the two founders of Blau-Weiss, saw how antisemitism had taken hold in a movement that was supposed to embrace nature and love of the land and turned it into a breeding ground for repulsion towards Jews. Blau-Weiss was launched as a Jewish alternative, and became a Zionist movement a decade later, in 1922.

Zionist youth movements started to flourish in Europe. Hashomer Hatzair, founded in Austria-Hungary in 1913, inspired by the Hashomer guardians of the Jewish pioneers in the Land of Israel, was founded as the first Zionist youth movement and has been active ever since. The trend of the *tnuot* kept growing: The Dror movement was founded in Poland in 1915, Betar in Latvia in 1923, Hanoar Hatzioni in Poland in 1927, Habonim in the United Kingdom in 1929, and others. Through Zionist movements, young Jews found a place where they could not only be proud of their own identity, but also develop it and allow it to grow.

It was during this period that the concept of the madrich was born. Tasked with the mission of inspiring their even younger scouts, or *hanichim*, on the Zionist path, while offering them lifelong skills and a personal connection with nature, Judaism, and the Land of Israel—the madrich became the role model for tens of thousands of young Zionists who formed the core of the movement that built the State of Israel.

Those who chose the path of the madrich were offering a circle of freedom for Jewish identity, both physically and spiritually. The movements, through the figure of the madrich, formed the core of the revolution in global Jewish identity that ultimately expressed itself through the establishment of Israel in 1948.

* * *

The role of the madrich represents the essence of Zionism for young Jews, and an invaluable legacy to all Jews. The madrich takes dreams to the highest level and works tirelessly to realize them, embodying the highest values of our people.

This is why I am a Zionist. Because my experience of the youth movements—in my case, Hanoar Hatzioni—has shown me how a crisis can become an opportunity, how through the hard times we will find an answer, and how we can openly defy our realities with idealism.

Especially in the wake of October 7 and the period of uncertainty and fear we have entered, it is essential that the Jewish world redouble its investment in youth movements and the concept of the madrich—so we can capture and pass on their passion, that our children may live with their values and learn with them. As Sergio Edelstein of the World Zionist Organization has written, "the educational conception that characterizes the tnuot noar gives them a peculiarity: the educational processes are entirely formative, experimental, and experience-based."

In the early twentieth century, the greatest challenge facing the early madrichim was to pave the way for those who would follow them in a rapidly changing world. Prior to World War I, Zionist youth movements introduced the concept of *halutziut*, or pioneering. This was not just about reclaiming the Jewish homeland, but also of fashioning a new Jewish character—one of courage, criticism, determination, hard work, and imagination. These qualities would define tnuot forever, and they continue to inspire young Zionists. Indeed, they are the unique qualities that define the Israeli and Zionist character today.

As a madrich, I'm deeply aware of the debt we owe to our forebears in the Zionist youth movements of a century ago. It was they who built a large part of our modern Israeli legacy; they who, with a clear vision, came to work and settle the land with their own hands and injected a powerful idealism into the lives of the Jews who built the kibbutzim, moshavim, cities, and towns of the *yishuv*—without which there would be no Jewish state today.

But the role of the madrich, the values that drove madrichim to act as personal examples, and the determination to realize ideals, were not limited to building the land. During the Holocaust, the Zionist youth movements of Europe decided not only never to surrender to the Nazis, but to resist actively. They offered crucial support for their communities, organizing *peulot* (activities) even inside the ghettos, resisting the Nazi darkness with education and responsibility. Many of the movements—including Hashomer Hatzair, Hanoar Hatzioni, and Dror—continued their work, supporting thousands of hanichim, organizing food and medicine for thousands of families, organizing workplaces within ghettos, and playing a central role in the uprisings—leading the resistance against the Nazis within the ghettos and the underground of the Partisans, and even clandestine Aliyah.

✳ ✳ ✳

During the COVID-19 pandemic, we were forced to ask ourselves about our relevance in the Jewish world, and to question our techniques.

Today the youth movements face the terrible crisis of October 7. They have played an instrumental role in helping the families of the hostages, as well as volunteering to support farmers and communities affected.

Madrichim have proven that it is possible to reach the hearts of countless young Jews through the principle of *personal example*. As we saw through history, they not only can make a positive impact within their youth movements, but also can create the necessary change, and take action when needed, in order to give light and hope for Jews everywhere.

If we succeed in empowering the madrichim, we will be able to empower the soul of the entire Jewish people.

2

Embrace Chosenness!

Oliver Anisfeld

I don't know whether you have noticed, but it seems that no matter how compelling our arguments are, no matter how just Israel's cause is, we just aren't cutting through. Since October 7, the facts have become clearer than ever, so there's less room for the lies to hide—yet so many still believe them.

Israel does everything that is demanded of it. It gives back land for peace and is met with terror, but the world says Israel needs to do more. Israel is faced with Hamas's genocidal massacre, and when the IDF responds in the most surgically precise way (unprecedented in the history of urban warfare), it's called "genocide." We point to our ancient connection to the land, and we are called "colonizers." Despite the now-overwhelming evidence demonstrating widespread support for Hamas's Nazi-esque ideology among Palestinians, any measure Israel takes for basic

Oliver Anisfeld is a media entrepreneur focused on influencing opinion through "edutainment." In 2016 he set up J-TV, a global Jewish YouTube channel that presents inspiring Jewish wisdom and ideas to both Jews and non-Jews and spreads the truth of Israel's cause. He also runs several other media channels and projects. He lives in London and studied History at University College London, focusing on the influence of the Hebrew Bible on America's Founders.

security and survival is considered a "war crime."

It isn't surprising that many hasbara activists feel like they are bashing their heads against a wall. I am sure there are people out there who are open to reason and will see the obvious merit of Israel's case. But will we ever cut through the vicious hostility to Israel that lies at the root of this ongoing conflict? It certainly seems that our current strategy isn't doing the trick. We need a serious rethink.

* * *

Recently I was chatting with a young British Muslim who is sympathetic to Israel. He told me that one of the main arguments he hears in Muslim circles is that Israel is a "phony state" because the Jews are meant to be a godly, religious people—and the secular, democratic values espoused by Israel's leaders seem to reject this. Now, I do not for one second want to find any virtue behind the arguments that excuse the appalling hatred leveled at the Jewish state, but I do think this comment should give us pause. Israel is surrounded by religious, God-centric cultures, yet our activism is focused on impressing a Western audience. Israel's neighbors are not impressed by democracy or international law or even groundbreaking technology.

October 7 was the day that brought all of Israel's cosmic battles into sharp focus more than ever before. The day was Simchat Torah, when we start reading the Torah anew. We went back to Genesis, the beginning. The most famous of all Torah exegetes, Rashi, opens his very first comment with a question (paraphrased): "Why did the Torah begin with God's creation of the world and not the first commandment? Because if the nations of the world tell the Jews they are thieves, foreign occupiers of a land not theirs, Israel will respond that God is the creator of the universe and He assigned it to the Jews." It seems like Rashi is saying that this is the *only* argument the nations of the world will find convincing. I do not think it was by chance that Israel read this message on October 7, 2023. I think it is the call of the hour. We should be clear to the world who we are—God's chosen people, chosen to articulate His moral vision for the world—and whose right to the land comes from God Himself.

Now when I propose this to some Jews, they go crazy. "Are you trying to inflame tensions even more? This will only further enrage our enemies!"

When I discussed this with YouTube's most popular rabbi, Manis Friedman, he pointed out the following: First of all, how are all our other arguments working out for Israel's PR? Again, they aren't cutting through. Second, it's too late, we have already been chosen—we didn't do it, it happened to us. And for much of the world, the revelation on Mount Sinai is something they believe in; so they already know there is something different about the Jews.

Part of the reason hasbara fails is because it is rooted in our frustration that the world treats us differently, with "double-standards," and we crave for the Jews to be treated as a nation like all others. But we will always be treated differently, because the world knows *we are different*. And the more we deny it, the more it frustrates them. But difference is not necessarily a bad thing that we should resist. Difference can be wonderful.

The Jewish people's divine mission in this world could be best understood by imagining a teacher in a classroom full of students. The Jewish people are meant to be God's appointed moral teacher, and the nations of the world are the students. When a teacher tries to act like one of the students, they simply take advantage. They bully the teacher, and chaos reigns—but they certainly don't treat the teacher like one of them. All that happens is the teacher and students both become frustrated.

I don't doubt that, historically, antisemitism came from jealousy of the Jewish people's chosen role. Even if it wasn't said explicitly, it was clearly a key driver. But our chosenness is an irreversible fact. We can't deny it even if we want to, and when we have tried to run away from it, the world has always pushed back.

So the solution is not for us to shy away from our difference, but for us to speak clearly, with the authority of a teacher in a rowdy classroom. It is the nations—the students—who need to revise their attitude towards us. You can be jealous of someone else's position, or you can be proud to partner with them and excited to play your own unique role in this great divine plan. But this can happen only when everyone speaks plainly.

***

While the antisemitism of the past was driven by jealousy of our chosenness, one thing has changed today. People are gradually realizing the moral emptiness of the ideologies and institutions they once put their faith in. This came into particularly sharp focus in the aftermath of October 7, which I also do not see as a coincidence. Whether it's academia, political leaders, celebrity culture, the media, or even religious culture—we are witnessing a severe shortage of moral leadership. Couple this with the unprecedented political and social freedoms most Jews have today, and we now have the perfect opening for the Jewish people finally to come into their global role.

Antisemitism also thrives, in part, on the Jews' being a mystery. How is it that the Jews are so successful despite the odds being stacked against them? How does such a small people, with such unique features, have such a wide influence? These mysteries feed into conspiracy and paranoia, and in previous generations we simply did not have the freedom or security to challenge them. But today we do. What about, instead of just "fighting antisemitism," we try to create "pro-semitism"? If the hate thrives on mystery, let's demystify! Jews sometimes feel the world is "out to get us," but, again, that could be understood as wanting to "get" us—to understand who we really are.

Since my teen years, I have been consistently blown away by the depths of wisdom and moral brilliance in our Torah and Jewish heritage. I have been amazed at how much Judaism has already transformed the world in the

global conversation of ideas. Today we have an unprecedented opportunity to take this to a radically new level.

In a world crying out for moral leadership, it's finally
time for us to provide it. Getting rid of antisemitism is only
the short-term prize of this approach. The real prize will be
greater than we can imagine.

3

Young Jews Are Finally Learning to Fight Back

Alissa Bernstein

Faced with an acutely stressful situation, we have three choices: fight, flee, or freeze. Since I was a young girl, I never really understood fleeing or freezing up. Maybe there's a neural connection that never quite developed, making me prefer head-on confrontation. Whatever the reason, I've always been a fighter.

It took me many years to discover that many people are not. When called to action, many freeze, conditioned to remain quiet to avoid retribution. This is particularly true for minorities who have been told both to put their heads down and to blend in if they wish to achieve success.

The Jewish community has been a prime example. After the Holocaust, standing out was not an option for most Jews, who came to the United States from countries that sought to exterminate or to ethnically cleanse them. Being loud in the

Alissa Bernstein is the Assistant Director of American Jewish Committee (AJC) Los Angeles, where she manages the region's political outreach, legislative advocacy, and interfaith and intergroup coalition building. Originally from Palo Alto, California, she graduated cum laude from Occidental College with a degree in Psychology and Spanish, where she spent her time advocating for Jewish issues and creating educational opportunities with the administration about campus antisemitism.

face of antisemitism meant putting oneself at risk.

It has been eighty years since the worst atrocity the Jewish people has ever faced, yet so many in our community have continued to freeze up in the face of anti-Jewish and anti-Israel hate. This is particularly true of the younger generation—my peers, who have been uncomfortable speaking out or identifying as Zionists in public.

I often wondered why. Perhaps we were grasping for some kind of self-preservation tactic, albeit temporary and, in my opinion, largely ineffective. Although the Jewish community has historically been at the forefront of societal change, particularly in the United States, in recent decades we have foregone advocating for ourselves for the sake of advocating for others, many of whom have little to no interest in doing the same for us. We have adopted ideologies that put us directly in harm's way for the sake of keeping our friends. We have often done this at our own expense, shaking off a public Jewish or Zionist identity to appease others.

I think this has been, in part, a result of a false sense of security. Many young Jews didn't recognize the real threats facing our community and Israel, not having lived during a time when they were threatened. We believed that through the success of the Zionist movement and our cultural assimilation in the decades following the Holocaust, we—and Israel—were untouchable. Thus, we helped create communities defined by ideology, and we ended up ostracizing ourselves from the very communities we had built.

Now we find ourselves caught in a maze.

Here's the thing. This false sense of security is just a symptom of a much deeper problem the Jewish community has faced for decades, and which has inspired conversation across denominations, practices, and cultural backgrounds. FBI statistics, after all, show that Jews have *not* been secure, as antisemitic hate crimes have tripled in the last three decades.

So where did Jews get the idea that they were so secure? The answer may have to do with their efforts to distance themselves from their cultural, religious, and traditional identity. This distancing may even have taken place *because*, in part, the Jews are known to be a historically targeted people. With each step away from their traditions, Jews believed they were becoming more secure, even when evidence suggested the opposite.

***

The United States population has become less religious in recent decades as a whole, and Jews are no exception. In the last decade alone—according to a 2020 Pew Research Study—Jewish denominational identity has moved towards larger participation in the Reform movement, and away from the once-dominant Conservative movement. The same study shows that American Jews are less likely to attend religious services than other faith groups in the United States. In fact, almost a third of American Jews don't identify with religion at all.

Nor is the distancing expressed only in terms of religion.

Only about a third of Jewish families send their children to Jewish summer camps, and the less religiously committed Jewish families are in this country, the less likely they are to send their kids to a Jewish school. As a community, we are distancing ourselves from the ancient sources of our unity and identity.

I was raised in a Conservative, Zionist, Jewish household that kept kosher, celebrated Shabbat every week, sent me to Sunday school and Jewish summer camp, and encouraged involvement in Jewish youth programs. Throughout the most formative years of my life, my strongest social networks were in Jewish spaces. Being raised in a home where Jewish history, culture, and tradition were celebrated, and having friends who had similar upbringings, cultivated a strong sense of Jewish and Zionist identity and a connection to the broader community. My upbringing is what made me an advocate; I understand that to love something is to fight for its strength and protection.

For many years I felt out of place among some of my Jewish peers—particularly those with whom I attended secular public school, who had vastly different Jewish upbringings from my own. Later, I noticed that Jewish friends from college who did not have a similar upbringing lacked a strong sense of Jewish identity, both as individuals and as part of a broader community. Many of them like to say they are "Jew-ish," like they are talking about the color of their hair—something they were born with but which could be easily changed. Often they are disconnected from, or adversarial towards, Israel and Zionism, and seem to have no interest in being advocates for either our community or our homeland.

In place of tradition and observance, which are incredibly important markers of our ethnic and historical background, many Jews see Judaism as simply a "culture." We have moved from Tanakh, Talmud, and Mishna to tzimmes, whitefish, and matzoh. Adopting the notion that we are simply a "culture" not only prevents us from understanding who we are in all of our beautiful diversity and depth, it also makes us less capable of educating others. As a result, we allow non-Jews to decide for themselves who they think we are—with the inevitable scapegoating that results. I believe we have come to an era of reckoning that is forcing us to accept that our generations of assimilation have done far more harm than good.

When I was ten, a classmate told me that he wanted to finish what Hitler started and to kill the rest of the Jews. I lived in a town with a strong Jewish community; to be Jewish was an immense source of joy and power. It came as a shock to learn that some people thought that being Jewish is bad—that the world should be rid of us.

* * *

When I started college, it didn't take long to discover how lackluster the campus Jewish community's relationship with Israel was. With close to one hundred active student clubs, two were Jewish, and one of them explicitly anti-Israel. That group dominated the campus discussion of Israel and had a knack for drowning out Zionist voices—so much so that when a group of Jewish students was publicly lambasted by the student body for speaking up against a terror attack in Israel, the administration demanded *they* apologize for their statement. Several of them were harassed and intimidated at events on campus for weeks to come.

Reeling from the antisemitism I watched spreading across my campus, I met with a coalition of concerned Zionist Jewish students who felt as enraged as I did. Yet, none of them felt these incidents warranted action.

I knew that if I wanted anything to change, I would have to do something. After graduating, I sprang headfirst into a career focused specifically on Jewish and Israel advocacy through the American Jewish Committee (AJC). According to the AJC's *State of Antisemitism in America 2023 Report*—which assesses and compares the Jewish and general population perceptions of, and experiences with, antisemitism in the United States—no fewer than 94 percent of American Jews feel antisemitism is a problem in the U.S. today. Since the Hamas attacks on October 7, 77 percent of American Jews feel less safe in the United States.

My peers have begun to understand the growing threat against our community, and many seem to have disabused themselves of the notion that we are in any way protected from antisemitism in contemporary society.

In the months since October 7, the Jewish community has been a punching bag for global rage against Israel—because, and only because, the Jewish state is defending itself. Many young Jews seem to be waking up to this fact; I see more Jewish pride, Jewish joy, and resilience than I could have ever expected. I see my peers demanding justice. I see the global Jewish community aflame with determination. Finally, my community is realizing that neither fleeing nor freezing will stop evildoers from attempting to destroy us.

So why, all of a sudden, is such a large part of the Jewish community so activated, determined, and resolute? What was it about the Hamas attack that triggered our *fight* response?

***

The myth of Jewish security has been shattered. Many young American Jews are witnessing a war which poses an existential threat to their homeland for the first time in their lives. On October 7, they watched as Hamas, an Iranian proxy, launched missile attacks in Israel's South, and brutally murdered and raped more than a thousand Jews. They watched as hundreds of civilians from Israel, America, Thailand, and many other countries were stolen away and taken hostage underground.

For the first time, young American Jews understand the threat that antisemitism poses not just to Israel, but to Jews around the world. For the first time, they are experiencing real, direct, and dangerous Jew-hatred. They see it in their social media feeds, on their campuses, in the media, and in their places of work. They finally understand that no matter how much they try to distance themselves from their Jewish or Zionist identities, our adversaries will threaten us all the same.

Today they realize that to be a Jew and a Zionist requires action. Many of the same people I knew to be quietly Jewish and Zionist before October 7 are now proudly wearing a yellow ribbon to raise awareness of the hostages, or a Star of David to feel more connected to their identity. Many of them are now educating their peers about the ongoing war. Many are also attending synagogue regularly, keeping Shabbat in a way that feels authentic to them, and seeking Jewish community wherever they can find it.

Since October 7, many young Jews have begun to identify with, and to feel a deepened connection to, their homeland. They understand that "Zionist" is not a dirty word, as we'd been taught by many of our non-Jewish peers. They understand that to be a Zionist is to fight hate actively, to stand up for our community, to educate our non-Jewish friends, and to shake off those who oppose our very identities.

Young Jews are waking up to the fact that simply being Jewish isn't enough to safeguard our people. If we want to see the Jewish people thrive, and if we want to protect and maintain the Jewish homeland whose neighbors want it gone, we must *practice* Judaism and Zionism actively. We must find ways to feel connected to our historical, traditional, religious, and spiritual roots, so that we feel capable of empowering and strengtheing our community for generations to come.

I am proud to watch my peers understand that to be a Zionist is to be a fighter for the Jewish people, a unifier, and an advocate. To be a Zionist is to stand up in the face of hate, to tell our adversaries that we will not cower, to show the world that we will not be destroyed. To be a Zionist is to tell the world that we always have been, and always will be: *Am Yisrael*, the people of Israel.

4

Why Mordecai M. Kaplan Matters After October 7

Oz Bin Nun

The October 7 massacre and the war that followed have made clear just how global an affair "Zionism" has become. Indeed, today the hatred of Zionism extends from Berlin to Brooklyn, from Dagestan to Durban, from Malmö to Morningside Heights. Thousands of miles from the Negev and the Galilee, in innumerable locations around the world, the word "Zionism" is injected with every imaginable evil. Seen up close, this hatred is immediate, palpable, and directed not just at Israel and Israelis, but at the Jewish people as a whole and anyone who identifies with it.

Indeed, it has become clearer than ever that this conflict is not limited to the territory "from the River to the Sea." Jews have become a frequent target, and the relative calm that once characterized life in the Diaspora, especially in the United States, has been shattered.

An earthquake has shaken the world—especially the

Oz Bin Nun is studying Psychology and Philosophy at the Hebrew University in Jerusalem. He has served as an emissary of the Jewish Agency at the University of Wisconsin, and is a graduate of the Bronfman Fellowships. A writer, content creator, and social activist, he served as a commander in the Egoz Commando unit in the 2023-2024 Gaza war.

Jewish world. This new era demands new forms of coping. It demands that we rethink fundamental assumptions, and that we ask: Who *are* the Jewish people after October 7?

***

The word "Zionism" has had different incarnations. At its core, it refers to a movement of the national return of the Jews to the Land of Israel and the establishment there of a Jewish state. This definition is practical, simple, and specific, but it doesn't cover the full meaning that this word contains within it, and certainly not the emotions it evokes.

The first step to understanding the current hatred of Zionism is to ignore the specific, pragmatic, Ben-Gurionite definition of Zionism. Not because David Ben-Gurion's vision failed, but the opposite: because it succeeded beyond all imagination. The hatred of Ben-Gurion's Zionism is like other hatreds in the Middle East, which refer to long-ago humiliations and defeats, to perceived historical injustice.

Today's global hatred of Zionism is different. It is a struggle against specific realities today, and it takes place for the most part far away from Israel, and against people who do not necessarily have Israeli citizenship.

In order to understand the place of Zionism today, we should begin with one attempt to redefine Zionism that began after Israel's founding.

In his 1955 book *A New Zionism*, Mordecai M. Kaplan, a founder of the Reconstructionist movement, offers a new definition of Zionism. The essence of his approach is that because a Jewish state has already been established, world Jewry must formally redefine itself. The founding of Israel required disconnecting from the supernatural belief in a miraculous messiah and freeing ourselves from the traditional beliefs in heavenly redemption, which included an exilic helplessness. In contrast, Zionists worked for rejection of the condition of exile.

Kaplan's proposal comes after the establishment of Israel, but embraces Zionism's intellectual core and applies it to the Diaspora. He points to the moment when Jews decide to disabuse themselves of illusions and to create what in the field of psychology is known as a "locus of control" for the Jewish community.

This "locus of control" is the sense a person may have about how events of his or her life are determined—what causes good or bad things to happen to them. Whether this is internal or external will determine whether people view themselves as sovereign over their lives, or project that control onto others. The importance of the first phase of Zionism, in Kaplan's approach, was not just in the practical achievment of establishing the state, but in emancipating the Jewish people from the passive belief in an external source of control, and replacing it with an active approach focused on internal control.

The "New Jew" of Zionism, in this view, is not different in posture or musculature, but rather in the ability to take responsibility for the lives of one's Jewish brothers and sisters. The Jews' refusal to abandon the blood of their people to the graces of the *goyim*, of history, or even of God, is the root of this internal locus of control. The biblical declaration *hineni* ("Here am I"), when other Jews are suffering, is the absolute core of the entire Zionist movement.

Today, the second phase requires that we be no less revolutionary in spirit. Today, Zionism must aim, as Kaplan puts it, "to reconstitute the Jewish people, to reunify it, and to redefine its status vis-à-vis the rest of the world." Kaplan calls on us to take responsibility over additional spheres of Jewish life beyond the State of Israel. In this sense, anywhere there is an established Jewish community, anywhere that Jews feel that they are responsible for the fate of their community—there is Zionism. This responsibility cannot be atomistic; the entire Jewish community is bound to each other for the same reason and in the same solidarity, and therefore the same decisive act aims at the unity of the community, demands of it its physical and spiritual renewal, and enables active and positive acts towards the world.

* * *

So, who opposes such an idea—and why?

For extreme Islamists, on the one hand, the very idea of Jewish solidarity, and especially the idea of an internal Jewish locus of control, is nothing less than a sin against God. The rise of the Jewish state in the Middle East, together with the prosperity and success of the people who—according to their view—are required to live under Muslim rule, is a finger in the eye of the faithful. This frustration is felt both towards Israel and towards Jews in general, as well as towards the West as a whole, because in all these cases we are talking about an intolerable reality from the Islamist point of view—one that must change immediately.

For extreme Leftists, on the other hand, the focus is on their understanding of Jews as privileged and white. From their perspective, any "oppressor" group that demonstrates internal solidarity is guilty of a cardinal sin. In the theology of the radical Left, the path to redemption for the white man begins with the acceptance of his guilt and subordination to the oppressed. Anything less is heresy—a rejection of the post-modern messianic vision. Zionism is thus a sin, not merely because of the State of Israel, but because of the very existence of the Jew who diverges from his or her sphere of white privilege. Acts of violence against those perceived as oppressed, and the justification of those acts—regardless of whatever complexity and nuance accompany them—are spitting in the face of their god. And any means necessary to resist them is justified.

In Western countries, where these forces command no armies, their main method of resistance is by commandeering the public discourse in an attempt to create a permanent state of confusion in which Jews cannot publicly identify with Israel without being rejected, attacked, and taken out of context. Every aspect of Jewish solidarity, including organizations like the Anti-Defamation League (ADL), are demonized. Any statement, no matter how complex or nuanced, is taken out of context and weaponized against the Jews. This leads to what Hannah Arendt called "the disappearance of the public realm"—a public inability to look together at the same reality.

This attack on Zionism, it should be noted, recognizes the enormous potential in Zionism's central idea: the power implicit in the ability of Jewish communities to support each other and to take mutual responsibility. Zionism in Kaplan's sense of the word allows that power to be understood at the communal level, and to influence reality at the political level. The internal Jewish locus of control returns to the Jews their ability to be understood, and therefore not to be alone.

To a large degree, Kaplan's Zionism is the way out of our predicament. Jewish solidarity is the one thing that can guarantee Jewish participation in the public sphere, in the long run, as well as internal Jewish engagement that has been in decline. There can be no hope for the Jewish people unless we learn to stand together against the onslaught—and we cannot do that without Jewish solidarity.

* * *

The central problem in today's Zionist discourse is its insistence on the Ben-Gurionite approach: focusing exclusively on the Jews' right to a sovereign state in the Land of Israel. During the current war, and with the best of intentions, with an awareness of the looming dangers and in the effort to steel ourselves against what is to come, the Jewish communities on both sides of the ocean try to revert to the comfortable clarity of early Zionism, and the implicit division of labor between the Israeli protagonist and the faithful supporting role of the American Jew. The shipments of military gear and warm clothes, the massive funds that crossed the Atlantic from West to East in the Fall of 2023 and Spring of 2024 were deeply appreciated and truly important—but not what the Jews *as a whole* actually needed.

This effort is not merely one-sided and unsustainable. It misses the key to the survival and prosperity of Jewish communities: the internal locus of control and the solidarity it implies. One cannot act as though the only important story is happening in Israel while taking care of one's local community at the same time. We must understand that there is a joint Jewish story, with significant existential challenges. Unfortunately, the dialogue taking place right now among Jewish communities is about how much aid to give and how, with an almost absolute focus on the Israeli story—leaving the American Jewish community in a passive stance of an external locus of control, leaving out the possibility of auto-emancipation and political self-actualization. In the long run, such a development will be devastating for *both* the Diaspora and Israel.

This passive inclination rests on another fundamental error. It must be said clearly that criticism of Israel, when it comes from the solidarity of fellow Jews, is both legitimate and welcome. Jewish communities are allowed to criticize Israel—just as Israel is allowed to criticize the Diaspora. Moreover, the emergence of a complex and nuanced discourse, which attempts to improve and remedy the faults of the world and to bring about positive change through mutual understanding—this is exactly what our people needs, now more than ever.

The problems begin when the basic assumption is that Jewish solidarity is inherently racist and therefore illegitimate, or that a Jewish state is an original sin and therefore the world can be made whole only by its disappearance. As soon as these are the assumptions, there can be no community or responsibility, only frightened individuals who are easily controlled by others.

***

So what, if we are to accept Kaplan's approach, is to be done? First, we must rehabilitate the Jewish people. That is to say, we must rebuild our ability to identify as Jews individually, to engage with the Jewish community, and most importantly, to see to it that Jews are physically and spiritually secure wherever they live. This challenge is more difficult than may seem, especially at a time when calls to "globalize the Intifada" are heard increasingly in American streets, and Jews feel afraid and under attack. Every Jew in the world, and every Jewish community, from Tel Aviv to New York City, should be willing to say "Here am I," and to take responsibility for their brothers and sisters.

Second, we must redefine the status of the Jewish people with respect to the rest of the world. We have to give up on the false binary that holds Tikkun Olam to be at odds with Jewish solidarity, to abandon the illusion that Tikkun Olam means self-cancellation in the face of the noisiest trends claiming the mantle of righteousness while in fact supporting terror and antisemitism. The Jewish community will have to find for itself a new story, one that comes from a perspective of Jewish unity, and through that to repair the world. Perhaps the best place to start is with the figure of Rabbi Abraham Joshua Heschel, who represented in his moral and courageous acts the political meaning of Jewish faith and commitment.

Finally, to "reunite." We will have to find the path to profound discourse among the different Jewish communities. We must let go of the illusion that Israel is the main actor, and American Jewry a supporting actor. American Jewry must reconstitute itself as a cultural and political community, to speak its mind, to take responsibility for its brothers and sisters, and to develop a profound and important dialogue with Israeli Jewry. Only in this way can we face the difficult times ahead of us and, to whatever extent possible, repair the world.

5

Our Urgent Search for New Allies

Talia Bodner

On the morning of October 7, when Hamas showed the world exactly what the rallying cry "from the River to the Sea" looks like in practice, that genocidal slogan took off like wildfire on college campuses around the world. Fewer than five days after the October 7 attack, before Israel had even begun a significant military retaliation, thousands of my peers at Columbia University flooded the campus to protest against Israel's right to defend itself—or more accurately, against Israel's right to exist.

Immediately, teachers and other adults on campus reassured me that, while the voices of the anti-Zionists and antisemites may be loud, they are not the majority, and in fact represent only a tiny fraction of the population as a whole.

Talia Bodner is a student from the San Francisco Bay Area who is studying in the Joint Program between Columbia University and the Jewish Theological Seminary in New York City, where she studies Jewish Gender and Women's Studies as well as Political Science. In the spring of 2023, she returned from a gap year on Young Judaea Year Course in Israel where she interned in the Knesset and volunteered teaching English to Israeli-Arab students in Tel Aviv. She performed spoken word poems at the November 14, 2023 March for Israel at the National Mall in Washington, D.C. and at the World Zionist Organization's 2023 Conference on Informal Education and Leadership in Jerusalem. She is also a blog author for the *Times of Israel.*

But while this might be the case for their generation, it does not feel true for mine. My parents and my friends' parents received messages of love and support from their non-Jewish community members, expressing condolences and condemnation of what happened to our Israeli friends and family. I, on the other hand, did not receive a single text from my non-Jewish friends. Not one.

On November 14, 2023, when I stood before hundreds of thousands of people and spoke at the March for Israel at the National Mall in Washington, D.C., I felt immense gratitude for the ability to be in the presence of so many Jews. And still, I felt a deep sense of dread. Because I knew that while I was surrounded by so many Jews, there were so few non-Jews standing with us. Everyone around me was so impressed at the non-Jewish allies who spoke up at the rally to condemn Hamas and to advocate for Israel's right to exist and to defend its people. And yet, all I could think was: *Not one of them is my age.*

***

In 2016, my Jewish friends and I marched in our pink hats alongside feminists from every generation and background. In 2018, I rallied with my peers from Jewish day school for gun safety, alongside students and their families from every school district and neighborhood. Then in 2020, my Jewish friends and I joined our African American peers in Black Lives Matter protests around the country.

My identity has been shaped by my efforts to be an

advocate, a friend, and an ally. In every movement of activism, I stood among friends of different races, religions, genders, sexualities, nationalities, ethnicities, and ages. But in November 2023, I looked around at my peers and found myself standing among Jews only. Now, in our moment of great need, young Jews were left advocating alone.

College is the place where young people have the opportunity to develop and solidify their opinions, where we learn to build up our voices to become strong leaders. People tell me again and again that while these anti-Israel protests might sound the loudest, they are not the majority. But if we don't act now, then they will be soon enough. And if we continue on this path, the voices yelling in colleges will be yelling in positions of authority in industry, in culture, and in the halls of government.

Children are taught nowadays to be neither a bully nor a bystander. My generation has been raised to be active *upstanders*; we are a generation bred for activism. So why, when an Israeli student on my college campus hangs posters of innocent civilians who are being held hostage, and then gets beaten with a stick, does no one stand up? Why, when a student posts on a school-specific social media platform, calling for all IDF veteran students to "die a slow and painful death," is it reposted, instead of reported? And why, when a Columbia student makes a video saying "Zionists don't deserve to live," or "Be grateful I am not just going out and murdering Zionists," do people not see why it's the least bit problematic?

Jewish and Zionist students on college campuses are

crying out for help, screaming into a void, only to be met with a tsunami of antisemitism and hate. The voice of young Jewish Zionists on campuses is louder than ever before, and still—in our generation of intersectionality, allyship, and activism—we Jews are left standing alone. And as more and more "woke" Jews turn against their Zionist brothers and sisters, we Zionist youth who are standing up for ourselves are left with no allies.

Sadly, it seems like we are the only ones noticing.

So how do we address what might be the single most important challenge for the young Zionist movement in America today: our lack of allyship?

* * *

One option would be to abandon our search for allies and to continue standing alone. We can adopt the bootstrap mentality of self-reliance: Only Jews are responsible for Jewish self-determination, autonomy, and auto-emancipation. And in some ways, when we do succeed, isn't it even more gratifying to know we were able to do it ourselves?

Perhaps. But that is a big risk that could have disastrous consequences if it is not effective. So while the Jewish people are a mighty nation, we are too tiny to overcome our challenges without allies. Just as Israel needs allies to stand alongside her in an international community that often seems out to get her, so too must we rely on the support of others to help us overcome the challenges of our adversaries. And that means we must continue to work to build allies.

So now the question is: What are we looking for in an ally? For starters, we need people who will amplify our voices rather than trying to speak on our behalf. But this, in turn, raises the question of how the beliefs and political opinions of potential allies affect our ability to collaborate with them on this issue. If we are truly going to recruit allies who will be there for us in our moment of need, then we must cultivate them from the Left and the Right, from both liberals and conservatives.

But that gets complicated, especially on campus. On the one hand, it has been reassuring to see leaders on the Right who have advocated for American support of Israel. However, as a progressive young woman, I often find it uncomfortable to be in conservative political spaces. I often have to check my other values at the door; I don't see eye-to-eye with them on so many other social justice issues like LGBTQ+ rights, gender equality, climate change, reproductive rights, racial equality, gun safety, and the separation of church and state.

Sometimes, I even question whether our conservative allies are really advocating for us for the right reason. I worry when leaders of the radical Right, some of whom have been known to promote antisemitism, support Israel's war against Hamas. Are they supporting Israel because they believe in the justness and morality of the Jewish state, or because they hate our enemies more than they hate us right now? What happens when the war ends? Can these leaders remain our allies when the radicals among them fall back into antisemitic tropes like "Jews will not replace us"?

On the other hand, even if we can maintain our relationships with the conservative Right, we may risk alienating our friends on the progressive Left. For years, we had allies on the Left because progressive leaders valued our intersectional identities; but now progressive intersectionality has begun to exclude not only Zionism, but more and more, it seems no longer to include Judaism either. When champions of social justice spew anti-Zionist and antisemitic hate speech in their efforts to delegitimize Israel, I find it hard to imagine a world in which we are ever able to rebuild those relationships. And yet, surely, we must try. Right?

✱ ✱ ✱

There was a time when we could engage in healthy discourse across the picket line, with diverse perspectives and opinions. When Israel and Hamas went to war in the spring of 2021, I was a junior in high school and the president of my school's Jewish Student Association. When my progressive friends would post slogans on social media that were hyper-critical of Israel, I found myself immersed in deep and difficult conversations about the complexities of the war, the nuances of the region, and the righteousness of Israel's struggle. After such conversations, my friends almost always stood by me.

Only three years later, in the wake of Israel's war against Hamas, some of those people who were once my closest friends won't talk to me. My high school best friend blocked me on October 7, the moment I posted "My heart is in Israel." It seems dear friends would now rather completely ignore me than have a conversation about our differences of opinion. So yes, it's disheartening and challenging, but I still believe we need to keep trying to find people willing to have the tough conversations.

Some of us will continue to reach out to our former allies on the progressive Left, and we need those people not to give up on those friendships. Others will turn to the conservative Right and attempt to build stronger relationships there—and we need those people to cultivate new allies as well. Still others will choose to go it alone, and we need those people's valiant efforts to continue to strengthen our collective resolve. The question of which path to take is arguably the hardest and yet most important choice every young Zionist will inevitably have to make.

The truth of the matter is, I have seen people with whom I agree 99 percent of the time willing to drop me on a dime over the one thing we can't agree on. And if I expect them to work harder at maintaining our friendship despite our differences, then I must be willing to commit to the same. It has become increasingly important to embrace the discomfort of disagreement in order to break the cycle of intolerance that our society has fallen into. We must be able to make space for people with opposing viewpoints and continue to engage them intellectually. And we have to remember that sometimes, we need to be able to check partisanship at the door so we can sit down and find our common ground.

Whichever path to allyship we decide to follow, one thing is clear: If we don't choose for ourselves, the decision will be made for us. And we will continue to struggle alone.

6

To Stand United, We Must Respect Our Different Paths

Ashira Boxman

While attending the March for Israel in Washington, D.C., on November 14, 2023—one of the largest gatherings of American Jews in modern history—I closed my eyes for a second and imagined how it might have felt for our ancestors standing at the foot of Mount Sinai.

Back then, according to Exodus, hundreds of thousands of Israelites, hailing from diverse tribes, came together for a collective purpose. These individuals knew in their hearts that this moment demanded their presence. Some arrived at this moment looking for hope, others sought inspiration, and still others yearned for comfort. Perhaps for

Ashira Boxman is a fifth-year rabbinical student on the New York campus of Hebrew Union College and the rabbinic intern at Larchmont Temple. Ashira attended Florida State University where she studied Family and Child Sciences and Social Work. Following graduation, she worked at the Hillel of Broward and Palm Beach, engaging Jewish students on campus; and at the University of Texas Hillel as the Birthright Israel IACT Coordinator. She has taught at the Religious School at Central Synagogue, worked as the Rabbinic Intern at Temple Shaaray Tefila at Bedford Corners, spent a summer as the Staff Engagement Supervisor at URJ Camp Harlam and completed a pastoral-care internship at Bellevue Hospital.

most, it was merely a longing for a sense of belonging and camaraderie. As they stood shoulder to shoulder, forming one enormous entity, their diversity faded into the background, and their hearts and souls were interwoven. At this moment, they were not Jews or Hebrews, but rather *bne yisrael*, the united offspring of Israel, bound together as one family unit. Standing in this diverse yet unified crowd, they realized that "Children of Israel" was more than just a name—there was a sacred purpose behind it.

Now it was my turn. Standing on the National Mall in Washington, surrounded by close to 200,000 Jewish people coming from all corners of the earth and from across the political and religious spectrum, shook me to my core. I was thrown back 3,300 years to Sinai. Yet it wasn't a dream. On that day in Washington, the Children of Israel again stood united.

But why did it take a massacre of Jews, the deadliest day for our people since the Holocaust, to bring us together for the first time in our lifetimes?

★ ★ ★

The following month, I traveled to India on a JDC Entwine Insider Trip. Entwine allows participants to explore diverse communities and global Jewish issues, emphasizing personal responsibility. In India, our group was enriched by the presence of the Jewish Youth Pioneers (JYP), a group of young Jewish adults who play a vital role in sustaining the local community. As we learned about their unique Jewish experience, we found countless parallels in our traditions and customs. It was heartening to realize that while I'm baking challah, lighting Shabbat candles, praying at synagogue, or engaging in discussions about Israel, my friend and past president of JYP, Sharon Samuel, is doing the very same thing in India.

"Being Jewish in India, we don't know many other Jewish people, and many people in India don't know who we are," Sharon told me. "After the October 7 massacre in Israel, people around the world were reaching out to offer security for our Jewish community. It's comforting knowing that someone Jewish in America or Israel is looking out for us just because we are Jews." This is the essence of Jewish peoplehood: a collective commitment to stand by fellow Jews globally, and not just in times of tragedy. It is driven by the principle of *ahavat yisrael*—the love for our people.

* * *

The book of Exodus tells of Moses's ascent to the summit of Mount Sinai, where God commands him to wait, as he is about to receive the Tablets containing the Ten Commandments. Yet, Moses's ascent would offer something additional. He received a profound gift atop that mountain: a sacred and unforgettable image of *bnei yisrael* in a panoramic view that encapsulated the essence of the Children of Israel. He witnessed the twelve tribes of Israel standing before him, arranged by family, each appearing so different from one another, yet all standing side by side, revealing the beauty of the Jewish people even with its differences. Our unique strength is precisely that: unity without uniformity.

Moses, his brother Aaron, Aaron's two sons Nadav and Avihu, and the seventy elders of Israel ascended, but only Moses went to the top. The others were left behind after being given strict instruction from Moses: "Remain here for us until we return to you." (Exodus 24:14)

Now imagine if Moses had appealed to God for Aaron, Nadav, and Avihu to join him atop Mount Sinai. All of them could have had the opportunity to witness the breathtaking panoramic view capturing the essence of the united, yet diverse, Children of Israel.

A medieval rabbinic legend portrays Moses and Aaron walking up the mountain with Nadav and Avihu walking behind them. Nadav and Avihu remark to one another, "When these two elders die, we will rule over the congregation in their place." (Yalkut Shimoni 361)

Why were they not permitted to stand alongside Moses, soaking in the beauty of our diverse yet united community, thus preparing to amplify it for the next generation?

A more ancient rabbinic legend sharpens the question further, outlining two fatal sins of Nadav and Avihu, which might have been avoided had they been given a chance to stand on the mountaintop—and which are strikingly familiar in our Jewish world today. The first was the "strange fire" they brought to the altar; the second was the sin of "not having taken counsel" with one another. (Leviticus Rabba 20:8)

Nadav and Avihu each brought his own fire, which seemed odd to the other. According to the legend, they brought what they were familiar with, creating a fire reflecting only what they knew and had learned growing up. Yet, in the process, each omitted essential ingredients that could have produced a more sacred fire that warmed them all. They were ignorant of how to ignite the sacrificial fire, because no one had shown them how.

Likewise, many contemporary Jewish communities—including the Reform movement of which I am a part—have mistakenly omitted some crucial ingredients in the education of the next generation, including our sacred purpose of being *bnei yisrael*. For decades now, so many liberal Jews have prioritized the mitzvah of Tikkun Olam—repairing the world—at the expense of other critical Jewish values, especially *ahavat yisrael*. We have forgotten that the latter is inextricable from the former. To repair the world without repairing oneself is to care about the suffering of others while neglecting one's own. Mending our relationships with our fellow Jews, taking responsibility, and supporting communities halfway around the world are essential.

As the famous verse from the Mishna suggests, "If I am not for myself who will be for me? If I am only for myself, then what am I?" (Avot 1:14) Or the passage in the Shulchan Aruch, the premier halachic code from the sixteenth century: "Any relative should be given preference to a stranger; the poor of his own house to the poor of the city at large; the poor of his own city to the poor of other cities; and the poor who dwell in the Holy Land to those who dwell in other lands." (Yoreh Deah 251:3)

Here, we witness the intersection of particularism and

universalism. However, as the sequence of these verses implies, our initial focus should be directed inward *before* extending ourselves outward.

"A universal concern for humanity unaccompanied by a devotion to our particular people is self-destructive," wrote the great Reform theologian Eugene Borowitz, "but a passion for our people without involvement in humankind contradicts what the prophets have meant to us. Judaism calls us simultaneously to universal and particular obligations." This was the aspirational goal of the Reform movement half a century ago.

Since then, however, Reform Judaism has not conveyed adequately enough, especially to the younger gener\ ations, the importance of peoplehood and the concern for our fellow Jews.

As the Orthodox theologian Joseph B. Soloveitchik explained in his book *Kol Dodi Dofek*, the Jews in exile settled in different lands, encountered different cultures, and adopted a wide array of dialects and modes of dress. In a sense, the Jewish people sprouted multiple heads. This immediately raises the question of whether such a multi-headed being truly retains a sense of unity. The test case is what happens when one head finds itself in pain or trouble; if the other heads also cry out and seek relief, then they all still belong to one whole.

Our motivation to repair the world comes from the realization that our diverse experiences hold value and have shaped each individual's journey.

✱✱✱

I grew up in a home that emphasized the importance of Tikkun Olam. I deepened this important value by attending Union of Reform Judaism camps my whole life, participating in NFTY EIE High School in Israel, and being the daughter of a rabbi who chose to become a Reform rabbi *because* of the movement's emphasis on Tikkun Olam.

I have also been fortunate to have had many other experiences which have taught me the value of *ahavat yisrael*. I attended a Modern Orthodox Jewish day school, served on the board of my campus Chabad as the social action chair, and currently I am serving as a JDC-Weitzman Fellow, which teaches the importance of caring for all our fellow Jews wherever they live. These experiences have led me toward the summit of the mountain to observe, to engage with, and to learn from the diversity of the Children of Israel.

I sincerely hope Jewish leaders will develop greater tolerance and begin genuinely engaging in the richness of diversity that is our people. They can begin by appreciating the diverse ways Jews practice Judaism. When each Jew is confident in who they are, they do not need to fear those who worship differently. They need not be confined to the "strange fire" of their own denominations.

✱✱✱

Nadav and Avihu's other sin was not taking counsel from

one another. Each brother brought his own offering without discussing it with the other. They had no desire to learn from one another. They missed an opportunity to appreciate each other's contributions, and their inability to collaborate ultimately led to their downfall.

I recognize this danger way too often in our world today. We isolate ourselves from the rest of the Jewish world when we are unwilling to engage with perspectives different from our own. Like Nadav and Avihu's strange fire, other people's ideas and truths might appear unsettling, but we must push ourselves to engage with others, however strange it might feel at first.

By bringing future leaders up the mountain and enabling them to see the beauty that is the mosaic of our people, they might be more open to listening and learning from one another.

God said to Moses: "Come up to Me on the mountain, and be there." (Exodus 24:12) As individuals in the Jewish community, we need truly to *be there*, even when it feels uncomfortable, even when we disagree. My prayer for the Jewish community is to lead with openness, to remain present with the sacred beings before us, to cultivate growth through listening and engagement, to embrace difference, to transcend judgment with kindness, and to replace assumptions with understanding.

7

Does Liberal Judaism Have a Future?

Ofer Chizik

It all started when the rabbi taught us that "women are the Evil Inclination." I was thirteen. A secular boy taking post-Bar Mitzvah classes at an Orthodox synagogue in Israel.

I had enrolled out of the belief that only there could I deepen my understanding of my Jewish heritage. But when the rabbi presented a Judaism that had no place in it for the women closest to me—my mother, my female teachers, my female friends—something in my identity snapped. For many years after, I took a step back from the Jewish world. For a decade I didn't set foot in a synagogue.

And then, almost by accident, came the revelation: During my Master's Degree studies, I visited Manhattan, where I discovered American Judaism, and in particular, the

Ofer Chizik is a journalist, Reform rabbinic student at Hebrew Union College, and Ph.D. candidate at the Ruderman program for Jewish American studies at the University of Haifa. He also writes and edits for *Yedioth Aharonoth*, focusing on foreign news, world Jewry, and interfaith relations. Ofer also served as the spokesperson and media director for Hoshen, the education and advocacy organization of the LGBTQ+ community in Israel, and as the spokesperson for a Knesset member. Ofer was also a reporter at GLZ radio, where he received two GLZ editor-in-chief radio awards for excellent journalistic work.

versions of it collectively known as "liberal Judaism."

It was a short trip: ten days that included an assignment to attend a Friday night service. That one assignment revealed to me my own Jewish identity. For it was there, in New York City, that I understood for the first time that there was more than one way to be Jewish. For the first time in a decade, I felt like I belonged in a synagogue.

Today, three years later, I live in constant fear that the amazing, profound Jewish identity I discovered might yet shatter completely—whether in Israel or in America.

***

The Jewish people faces immense challenges in the coming decades, but I think the greatest of all is the preservation of Jewish identity. Not the arcane, regressive version I encountered at the age of thirteen, which discriminates against women and LGBTQ+ people. I am referring instead to the Jewish identity in its most basic and vital aspects—connection to the Jewish people, and an understanding of why it's important to be Jewish at all.

I look at my Israeli friends: Most of them are ultra-secular, completely disconnected from Judaism. They won't go to shul on holidays, some of them won't even join a Seder on Passover. Their weddings will surely be officiated by an Orthodox rabbi, because "that's how it's done." But they won't understand the text or ceremony, and it won't bother them that they don't. They're Jews because they live in Israel, but in substance, their identity or connection to Jewish identity means little to them.

At the same time, I look at my American friends—educators and rabbis who were trained to transmit Jewish knowledge to future generations. The sad truth is that their audience is dwindling. Fewer and fewer Jews in North America understand why it's important to be Jewish.

In Israel, the challenge is clear: Everyone here is taught from birth that Judaism is something binary—either you lead an Orthodox Jewish life, or you choose secularism, utterly devoid of Judaism. There's really no middle ground: Even Israeli traditionalism ("masorti") is defined through an Orthodox lens.

When we are never exposed to synagogues that don't discriminate against women; when we have no public transportation on Shabbat; when we're not allowed to have *hametz* in hospitals during Passover, even discreetly; when they tell us how to hold funerals, Bar Mitzvahs, and weddings; when Jewish identity is expressed through compulsion—how can anyone who believes in freedom and equality feel close to it? It is in the Jewish state that we are most forcibly pushed away from Judaism; it is through the Jewish state that our already small Jewish people is made even smaller.

Meanwhile in America, things are no less complicated. Just as we in Israel are pushing Jews away, in America the Jews themselves are pulling away. The sad fact is that whereas the synagogue was once the central institution for cultivating Jewish identity, few Jews still attend; "Jews of No Religion" are becoming increasingly prominent in

America. Jewish education in America, whether day-school or after-school programs, is often prohibitively expensive. Parents feel less connected to their Jewish identity, less connected to their community or synagogue, less connected to their faith—and their children even less so.

No less troubling is that fewer and fewer American Jews, especially among the younger generation, feel a connection to Israel. This connection, however, is crucial for global Jewry not just because of Zionism, but because Israel has been a major factor in preserving and building Jewish identity in the Diaspora over the last three-quarters of a century. The fact that the younger generation is growing apart from Israel means one more anchor of identity will weaken in the coming generations.

Of course, after October 7 all this became more complex. Alongside the many horrors there came a miracle: Our brothers and sisters around the world mobilized to support Israel, in an incredible display of responsibility and solidarity. Within the first month, it is estimated, nearly a billion dollars were raised. Since then, the number of American Jews also taking part in communities and Jewish activities has been rising, and in Israel, too, there's a rise in the number of young people wanting to connect with "something Jewish."

The danger, however, is that this may be fleeting. The anti-religious and anti-peoplehood trends in the United States are still felt in liberal spaces; in Israel, Orthodox compulsion directs young Jews to participate in only a very specific kind of Judaism. You can't build a strong liberal Jewish identity on the back of a single catastrophe; without a coherent set of values, without a strong connection to Israel, without a developed and unified ideology—this storm may only serve as a temporary cover for our endemic weakness.

Moreover, October 7 proved that the challenge of religious-national extremism is as strong as ever. In order to survive as a religious movement, we need to have a response. What is our liberal-Jewish answer to Islamist-nationalist violence? What are the limits of our liberalism? How far can we push the envelope in a way that preserves our identity both as liberals and as Jews?

* * *

At the heart of this crisis lies the fact that, even after nearly two centuries of liberal Judaism, we still haven't figured out how to fashion a unified heart in our liberal-Jewish identity: a uniform set of values, and possibly a uniform set of practices. In the Orthodox camp, it's clear who's in, who's out, and how to be in or out. These principles are discriminatory and hurtful, and I don't want to live by their light. But it's easy to preserve Jewish identity when you pray three times a day and marry only other Jews, because you're obligated to. It's easy to stay Jewish when others are defining "Jewish" for you.

We have chosen a harder path. We believe more in the journey than in the destination, and as such we have neither the ability nor the desire to tell others how to live. Free choice and individualism are the fundamental basis of our Judaism. We have taken it upon ourselves to be tested always and constantly—so that people will follow our path out of choice rather than inertia or compulsion.

In Israel, however, this approach is destined to fail. The lack of a separation of church and state results in a built-in weakness, and what we offer is insufficiently compelling to compete with the Orthodox propaganda aimed at us. Most secular Israeli Jews are not only unfamiliar with liberal Judaism, they have been indoctrinated into antagonism. In America, on the other hand, the situation is no better; the younger generation distances itself from Judaism. For them, too, what we offer is not sufficiently compelling to preserve the centers of Jewish strength—synagogues and communities.

As early as the foundational Pittsburgh Platform of 1885, "justice" and "righteousness" formed a central part of the liberal-Jewish theology, which with time took on the broader framing of Tikkun Olam. To be clear, Tikkun Olam is rightfully a central basis of our liberal-Jewish identity. But there are additional bases which we have neglected to a significant degree. Today, they seem to be missing in our effort to forge a liberal-Jewish identity that can stand the test of time.

What is to be done? At the level of ideas, we need to draft more explicit principles and to communicate them publicly—a vision along with policy, which express themselves in praxis that affects ordinary people: equality for women, for LGBTQ+ people, for minorities, free choice and free belief—these must remain central to our outlook.

But we need to understand what exactly are the core

values that stand behind these principles. Over the generations, our agenda has evolved: At first, liberal Jews like Rabbi David Einhorn fought for an end to slavery. Later we fought for the rights of immigrants and workers, and after that for the civil rights of African-Americans, and later for gay rights. Today we fight against the structural injustices across society as a whole.

On the one hand, evolution is necessary. History changes, and with it change the evils we face. The mandate of the Pittsburgh Platform, "to solve, on the basis of justice and righteousness, the problems presented by the contrasts and evils of the present organization of society," must be preserved. But on the other hand, we have seen that when we run after every cause without testing it against a defined set of values, we risk confusion, enmity, and sometimes even the enabling of antisemitism.

***

Our vision, therefore, must place a greater emphasis on boundaries—not to exclude, but to preserve. These boundaries ought to be very broad, but they have to be finite. In the American context, it is essential that we demonstrate greater commitment to Israel, the Jewish people, and the Hebrew language.

We must find new paths to reach our audience. Though I truly hope this is not the case, we may have to admit that the golden age of the American synagogue is over. In Israel, we may have to admit that we'll never break through just by building new congregations. We must pull together to rethink the question of how to reach our natural audiences anew.

We must also educate: In Israel, to expose the younger generation, from early years, to the third way, the liberal-Jewish way; in America, to show young people the blessings and the importance of peoplehood. And we must find innovative ways to connect liberal Jewish youths in Israel with those in America. This will require resources, and above all taking initiative and responsibility for our people.

The challenge is immense, and our opponents are many. From Jewish anti-Zionists, who do not understand that Jewishness is based also on solidarity; to so many Orthodox Jews who want to reject millions of Jews because one of their grandparents was, God forbid, not-entirely-certifiably Jewish. And those are just the rivals from within.

It is complicated to build a liberal-Jewish future. But we must try—if not for the future of the Jewish people, then at least for the thirteen-year-old boy who just wanted to learn something about his own heritage.

8

Instead of Fleeing Top Colleges, Stay and Fight

Adela Cojab

The concern for Jewish safety on college campuses did not begin on October 7, 2023. Back in 2019, I experienced firsthand the burgeoning wave of antisemitism at New York University (NYU).

It began with a statement from NYU's Governance Council for Minority and Marginalized Students equating Zionism with Nazism. As a member of NYU's Student Senate, I attempted to engage in dialogue with the council, only to be rebuffed and labeled a fascist for my Zionist identity. This was the first time my Zionism kept me from a space in which I was previously welcomed.

Adela Cojab is a lawyer, activist, and media contributor. In 2019, she filed the first-ever Title VI Complaint against NYU for failing to protect Jewish students from harassment during her time as an undergraduate. Her work—from political advocacy to interfaith peace rallies—has been recognized internationally, earning her designations as one of Hadassah's 18 Zionist American Women of 2024, Jewish Week's "36 Under 36," and JNS's Top 40 Latin-American Pro-Israel Advocates. She cohosts the interfaith podcast *Americanish: Daughters of Diaspora* and, as of 2024, hosts the OpenDor Media show *TodayUnpacked* on YouTube. She holds a J.D. from the Benjamin N. Cardozo School of Law and a B.A. from NYU's Gallatin School of Individualized Study, with a concentration in Middle Eastern Diaspora Structures.

The Jewish community gathered in response to draft a statement—not driven by anger, but disappointed, hurt that our peers would not take the time to understand why their comparison was so offensive to our community. The night before the statement was to be made public, a mentor advised me against publishing, suggesting that drawing attention to the issue would only exacerbate it. Fearing that he might be right, I made the difficult decision not to go public. It is one of my greatest regrets as an activist.

Our silence did not quell the rising tide of antisemitism. Instead, it allowed it to flourish unchecked, setting off a series of exclusionary and hostile actions against Jewish students on campus. Over the next few months, NYU's Jewish community saw multiple "Boycott, Divestment, Sanctions" (BDS) resolutions led both by student groups and members of NYU's faculty. Jewish students were targeted both in class and on social media. Events hosted by the Jewish community were frequently met with protests from the Students for Justice in Palestine (SJP) chapter, creating an environment of fear and intimidation.

I met with members of NYU's administration week after week, begging for action, worried for Jewish student safety.

The situation reached a critical point during the 2019 Yom Ha'atzmaut celebration, when an anti-Israel student protestor approached a group of Jewish students, Israeli flag in hand, and set it on fire. The protest continued, chanting "No Zionists at NYU," until another anti-Israel student approached the center during the singing of "Hatikvah," grabbed the microphone from a Jewish girl, injuring her in the process, and shouting "Free Palestine!" At that point, we looked up and saw they had torn our Israeli flags to shreds and hung them from trees and lampposts. NYPD stepped in and made arrests for property theft and damage, reckless endangerment, and assault and battery.

But while the police responded to these blatant acts of violence, the university turned a blind eye. Instead of taking action, they honored SJP with the President's Service Award, the highest honor a group can receive on campus.

This prompted me to pursue legal action against NYU. At the time, Title VI of the Civil Rights Act did not include Judaism under its protections. My case at the time had no legal teeth, but it caught the attention of the White House. Months after filing my case, in December 2019, I was invited to speak alongside President Donald Trump, and three days later, he signed an executive order expanding the definition of Jewish identity from a purely faith-based religion to an ethnicity or race, thereby falling under Title VI protections for ethnic minorities.

The executive order accomplished two significant breakthroughs. First, it conveyed a clear message to university administrators that Jewish students are entitled to the same safe and supportive campus environment as all other students, compelling educational institutions to recognize and address antisemitism with the same rigor applied to other forms of discrimination. But, more importantly, the executive order empowered Jewish students by affirming that their voices were both valuable and impactful. It demonstrated that when Jewish students advocate for their rights, they can effect meaningful change and affirm their place within the broader societal fabric.

***

In the wake of the October 7 events, the most common question I receive is whether Jewish students should co tinue to attend these schools. My unequivocal answer is Yes. Not only should we continue to send Jewish students to these institutions, but it is our responsibility to do so. To understand why, we need to view campuses as microcosms of society, and to see what we stand to lose should we choose to cower.

Reflecting on my time at NYU, I often think about the advice from my mentor, who suggested that drawing attention to antisemitism would only make it worse. This perspective, ingrained in the mentality of Jews of past generations, grounded in fear and caution, reflects a historical approach to Jewish identity.

Throughout history, being Jewish has rendered us distinct, and this distinction has often made us targets. In times of danger, Jewish communities were typically presented with only two options: conceal their identity or flee. This dichotomy of concealment or flight is a shared experience among Jewish communities, whether from Eastern or Western Europe or the Middle East.

However, the Jews of today are different, because we have a homeland of our own. While a homeland may seem to Jews in the Diaspora like a security blanket that encourages flight, we must understand our homeland differently: not as a contingency plan, but as an anchor for Jewish strength and identity. Israel symbolizes that Jews are no longer perpetual guests, but rightful citizens with the same rights and responsibilities as anyone else. The mere existence of the State of Israel reinforces our ability to assert our identity wherever we are.

It presents a third option: *to stay and fight.*

In popular culture, Jews are seldom depicted as fighters; instead, they are often portrayed as doctors, lawyers, entertainers, and bankers. Nevertheless, Jews have historically been at the forefront of the struggle for civil rights across the Diaspora, particularly in the United States. The historical commitment of Jewish activists to justice for all has helped to secure the rights of others in their respective societies, yet it raises a pressing question: Why, when our own rights are imperiled, are we so reluctant to stand our ground and fight to preserve those rights we have strived so hard to attain? Why is it that we, who have long championed the rights of others, are now so hesitant to advocate for ourselves?

This is the question we're really asking when we wonder whether to continue sending Jewish students to prestigious academic institutions.

And my unequivocal, resounding answer is Yes.

The panic of pulling our children from secular colleges is akin to the fear-driven reaction of making Aliyah at the first sign of danger. This response, while understandable, is both misguided and weak. It represents an instinctive retreat in the face of adversity, a concession to those who seek to marginalize and silence us. If this is what's happening in universities, where we have a hard-won seat at the table, what happens when we willingly step out of the room? Allowing others to dictate where Jews can and cannot feel comfortable is a surrender to antisemitism.

We should not deny ourselves the opportunities we deserve because our mere presence is disagreeable to others. We cannot allow institutions that preach societal inclusivity to be, in fact, inclusive of all *except Jews*. Jewish students should feel empowered to attend any university and pursue any field of study despite fear of discrimination. We must assert our right not only to survive, but to thrive. The territory we stand to lose is the hard-won progress in civil rights and societal integration we fought so hard to attain.

Next comes the issue of perpetuating the cycle of self-isolation. When parents decide to withdraw their children from academic institutions into which they have worked hard to gain admission, they inadvertently teach them that Jews do not belong where they are not welcomed. This instills fear in their children—the Jewish students of today who will become the Jewish parents of tomorrow. And, if Jewish students are not attending these institutions, the non-Jewish students who do attend—the leaders of tomorrow—will never meet their Jewish counterparts. This cycle of self-isolation, even self-ghettoization, begins with leaving colleges and continues with withdrawing from political and professional life. Denying ourselves participation prevents the normalization of Jewish presence, which is crucial for fostering understanding and inclusion.

If we do not allow ourselves to participate in these circles, how can we expect them, and the leaders they cultivate, to welcome us?

No, the answer to these questions—whether at universities, in professional circles, or in culture and the arts—is neither fright nor flight. Instead, stay and fight.

* * *

I sued NYU to ensure that no other *NYU student* would need to endure the discrimination that my friends and I faced. I had no idea my case would make national headlines, let alone contribute to a change in the application of civil rights protections and serve as a cornerstone for the proliferation of Title VI cases now being filed against Harvard, Columbia, the University of Pennsylvania, and others. A single voice makes a difference—but until we raise that voice, we cannot expect to be heard.

The Jewish Diaspora is far from dead; it is given life through the strength and resilience of those who refuse to bow to antisemitism. It thrives in students who stand against hatred and in the unwavering commitment to Jewish identity and pride, and they must do so, not only for their sake but for the sake of the Jewish future. The Diaspora will flourish as long as we remain steadfast in our resolve to fight for our rights and to assert our place in society. By standing up, we honor our heritage, secure our future, and demonstrate that the Jewish Diaspora is vibrant, resilient, and enduring.

The Diaspora is not dead, and if we fight for it, it will be here to stay.

9

The Duty of the "Inconspicuous" Jew

Charlie Covit

"I've heard different things from a lot of different people."
A few months after October 7, I was engaged in a
heated conversation with a Harvard professor. The topic at
hand? Just how bad the antisemitism problem was on our
campus in the wake of Hamas's attack.

The professor, a Jew himself, responded to my assertion
that the bigotry at Harvard had become overwhelming. He
was careful not to deny the problem; he acknowledged that
it was significant and that it needed to be dealt with. He
did want to note, however, that he had spoken to plenty of
other Jewish students who, apparently, had not experienced
any antisemitism at all.

I have no doubt the professor was correct.

Charlie Covit is a sophomore at Harvard College planning to study Modern Middle
Eastern studies and Economics. He is a Canadian citizen who grew up in New York
City and spent his gap year living in Jerusalem. Charlie speaks Hebrew fluently and can
read and write Arabic. He has also spent time volunteering in the Palestinian Territories
of the West Bank, studied Arabic in Morocco, and has traveled extensively throughout
the Middle East. His work has been published in the *Harvard Crimson*, the *Wall Street
Journal*, *Newsweek* and *The Times of Israel*'s blogs, and he has appeared on CNN, Fox,
Newsweek, and more.

As a non-Israeli, non-Orthodox Jew living in the United States in the twenty-first century, blending in is pretty easy for me, too. My name is Charlie Martin Covit. Some say I "look Jewish," but among the other guesses I've heard are Iraqi, Trinidadian, and Moroccan. I've spent time in Palestinian-controlled Bethlehem and Hebron and traveled throughout the Middle East and North Africa without anyone so much as suggesting I may be a Jew.

After October 7, when cheers of "globalize the Intifada" and "by any means necessary" echoed through Harvard Yard, I did not need to care. I could have chosen to stay silent, to go about my life, and not to concern myself with a war raging half a world away.

While that's not what I did, I do not resent those who made that choice—if anything, I am privileged to know I had the option, too.

* * *

I was recently engaged in a casual conversation with another Harvard student, bonding over our shared identity as Canadians, when I happened to mention that I was Jewish. "Oh, well are you a Jew *for Palestine?*" When I said no, she responded, "interesting," and walked away.

The moment stung, but in the days after, I also felt a pang of guilt. I never needed to have told her who I was. But for the Jews who have no "opt-out" button, the world sees them as Jews whether they like it or not.

The truth is that however extensive the antisemitism at

Harvard may be, my Israeli friends here have it far worse. Aside from having friends and family at war, Israeli students have seen themselves abandoned at dining hall tables and excluded from social clubs. They dread the classic college ice-breaker question of "where are you from?" knowing that glares will follow. They are forced to become defenders of the State of Israel in a court of public opinion that does not ask whether they want the job.

Meanwhile, my yarmulke-wearing friend has been harassed, belittled, screamed at, and followed—before even completing a single year at Harvard.

The fact that other Jews may have it easier is no consolation to them.

* * *

A couple weeks before that conversation with the professor, I was having lunch with my cousin Gila, when I noticed her Magen David necklace and asked her, half-jokingly, whether she wore it on her daily commute by train into New York City. "Of course," she replied. "Why should Orthodox Jews have to bear all the hate themselves?"

I, for one, had always worn my Star of David beneath my shirt, especially on the subway. That just felt like common sense. To Gila, however, common sense led her to do the exact opposite. She was opting *in*.

It was then that I realized that I, as a Jew who can pass as a Gentile, have a choice to make: Do *I* want to opt in? Do I want to wear my Magen David over my shirt on the subway, to go on CNN to say that my university is experiencing a crisis of antisemitism, and to wear my *kippa* on the way to Shabbat dinner on Friday nights? I'm certainly under no obligation, or even pressure, to do so.

Yet if the months since October 7 have taught me anything, it is that we, the "inconspicuous" Jews—*we must lean in*.

Today, it is Israelis who bear the brunt of abject hate, and Harvard students know that explicitly going after Jews would cross a red line. It's a dynamic that recalls the aftermath of the Bolshevik Revolution in Russia, when the newly formed USSR declared its enemy to be "Zionist, bourgeois Jews in capitalist countries," whereas Jews with a "Soviet Yiddish culture" were recognized as a nationality by the state. While it was not long before Joseph Stalin escalated the rhetoric and ordered the total destruction of Soviet Jewish cultural life, those Jews who chose not to call themselves Zionists enjoyed a relative degree of safety.

I share the example of the Soviets not because I believe—as did the Refuseniks who stood fast with their Jewish identity and their Zionist beliefs—that eventually, the evil will come for all Jews, Zionist or not.

At the same time, I do not believe that antisemitism alone should be the impetus for Jews to embrace who we are.

So while it may be true that for now it is the Israelis, and it could be any of us next, let us come together not because we fear what is to come tomorrow, but because our brothers and sisters are under threat *today*.

Jews are, at least in my view, the world's most awesome extended family. We've stuck together even through an exile that saw us scattered to Bucharest and Baghdad and everywhere in between. The fact that Ashkenazi Jews who lived along the Dnieper and Mizrahi Jews who settled by the Euphrates are closer genetically to one another than to their own Gentile neighbors is an almost unfathomable testament to the millennia-long connection between us. We have to look after each other.

＊＊

We are in a strange moment. Israel is under unprecedented threat, and antisemitism is soaring around the world. And yet, this isn't 1930s Germany: Nobody is checking whether anyone has a Jewish grandparent, and most Jews can go about their lives in relative safety.

The thing is, my professor was right. If we choose to, most of us really can live our lives without the word "antisemitism" even crossing our minds.

Emma Lazarus declares in her 1883 *Epistle to the Hebrews*:

> I do not hesitate to say that our national defect is that we are not "tribal" enough; we have not sufficient solidarity to perceive that when the life and property of a Jew in the uttermost provinces of the Caucuses are attacked, the dignity

of a Jew in free America is humiliated.
We who are prosperous and independent have not sufficient homogeneity to
champion on the ground of a common
creed...the rights of the lowest and poor-
est Jew-peddler who flees, for life and
liberty of thought, from Slavonic mobs.

Lazarus's repudiation of those Jews who choose not to concern themselves with the fate of their brethren feels poignant
in an era of soaring antisemitism that many Jews—particularly those willing to "refute" the connection between their
Judaism and Israel (as the filmmaker Jonathan Glazer infa-
mously did at the Oscars)—nonetheless feel they can avoid.

But Lazarus took care to remind, even demand of, the
Jewish people: "Until we are all free, we are none of us free."

The Jewish people are, fundamentally, an incredible
national family. And when it's your family that's in danger,
you don't keep your head down.

Now, more than ever, we all must lean in.

10

Jews Are Different. Time to Embrace It

Josh Feldman

The first time I watched *Fiddler on the Roof*, I hated it. It was, to my thirteen-year-old mind, pointless and boring. Nevertheless, despite my initial dislike for the film (which has since matured into a deep appreciation for the wonderful production that it is), I immediately took a liking to the song "Tradition"—mainly because I found it funny. But for Tevye, its narrator, it was far more than an entertaining singalong. Rather, it was symbolic of all the customs that have for generations sustained the Jewish people—and set us apart from everyone else.

Different communities throughout the Jewish world consider different aspects of Jewish life simply not to be questioned—be it marrying a Jewish spouse, keeping a kosher home, or attending each year's Passover Seders. But for many younger Jews today, perhaps the most central element of all—the idea that there is value in actively engaging with one's Jewish identity and community—has been anything

Josh Feldman is a Melbourne, Australia-based writer who focuses primarily on Israeli and Jewish issues. His work has appeared in English and Hebrew in the *Daily Beast*, *Newsweek*, the *Forward*, the *Sydney Morning Herald*, the *Australian*, Ynet, and *Makor Rishon*, among other publications.

but a given.

Indeed, the question of youth engagement has been the most recurring topic in my conversations with Australian Jewish communal leaders in recent years. How can organizations bring younger people to their events? How can we get university students to *shul* on Shabbat? Anyone involved in Jewish communal spaces will be acutely aware of such discussions. Few, however, have found a solution.

The October 7 massacre changed everything.

There were many layers to the shock that reverberated through the Jewish world on that Simchat Torah. From the inability to comprehend Israel's military failure, to the intergenerational trauma aggressively triggered by the deadliest day for Jews since the Holocaust, the Jewish soul was shattered. But for many Jews previously uninvolved in their communities, there was also a sudden awakening. As one childhood friend—whom I struggle to recall ever previously mentioning Israel or Judaism—told me three months after the massacre, "I've never been prouder to be Jewish."

He's not alone. A November Chabad.org survey of Chabad rabbis across the United States found that fully 77 percent of respondents said that since October 7, "they have seen a stronger sense of 'Jewish pride and confidence' among community members"; 86 percent reported that "community members have been experiencing a 'deeper connection to their own Jewish identity'"; while 93 percent said they were "witnessing a stronger feeling of 'connection to the Jewish people or desire to connect to other Jews' among community members."

The question for Jewish communities now, of course, is how to keep these Jews, who've suddenly discovered a love and care for the Jewish people, engaged in the long run. To allow this burst in Jewish pride to be a passing fad would be a betrayal of this pivotal moment in Jewish history.

The answer, I believe, lies not in doubling down on funding Israel programs, nor ramping up Israel advocacy, nor a myriad other initiatives that have been suggested. Rather, the key lies in changing the story the Jewish world tells about itself—in other words, being honest with ourselves about who we are.

The secret lies in one word: *different*.

* * *

Whether they consciously realize it or not, the atrocities of October 7 and the ensuing global explosion in Jew-hatred have reminded Jews the world over what many had forgotten: We are different. While for generations we had continued to marry within the faith and to keep generations-old traditions, a great many of us had told ourselves a lie that, at the end of the day, we were just like everyone else. We lived in the same neighborhoods as everyone else, went to the same universities, and worked alongside them five days a week. We convinced ourselves that we had finally achieved what our ancestors could only dream of: full acceptance into non-Jewish society; permission from the outside world to live just like everyone else.

But the problem, as Dara Horn, author of the bestselling book *People Love Dead Jews*, recently told me when I interviewed her for the *Australian Jewish News*, is that "Jews spent three thousand years not being like everyone else."

Ignoring such a salient fact about Jewish peoplehood has come at a great cost. Any successful individual or organization needs a *why*. Companies need to know why they exist and why consumers should buy their product, just as athletes must have an answer for why they put themselves through years of grueling training.

So too, does a strong Jewish identity need a *why*. Why be Jewish? Why be Zionist? Why actively engage with your Jewish community? For some, the answer is obvious, but for many, it's not. This is where we have failed younger generations. After all, if the implicit message we've been given is that we are just like everyone else, then indeed, why be Jewish?

It's that post-October 7 realization that Jews are not like anybody else, nor are we supposed to be, that has been behind this surge in Jewish engagement. As Liel Leibovitz wrote in *Jewish Priorities*, the realization that "Jews are outsiders" is in fact "the source of our moral courage and, paradoxically, the engine of our survival." In today's world, where fitting in is for many a grand aspiration, accepting that Jews are eternal outsiders may seem counterintuitive. But as Leibovitz explains, Jews "persist because we adhere to a different set of ideas, ancient and brilliant and true. When we do, we thrive."

This difference inherent to Jewishness is what has sustained us for thousands of years. Once we internalize that we are distinct from all other peoples and are the heirs of a beautiful, three-thousand-year tradition, and we accept those as good attributes, then the incentive for engaging with our Jewish identity is clear. After all, our Jewishness—whatever that may look like—is making us an offer that can't be found anywhere else.

If we want future Jewish generations to thrive, we need to hammer this message home: in schools, in shuls, in youth movements, in Jewish communal organizations, and particularly among newly engaged Jews. We're different, and that's okay. It doesn't make us any better or worse than others. In fact, it's great; it's what makes being Jewish so wonderful.

* * *

Unfortunately, Jews tend to remember our outsider status only at times of heightened antisemitism. "We can never be just Dutch, or just English, or whatever, we will always be Jews as well. And we'll have to keep on being Jews." Those words were written by Anne Frank, less than four months before her arrest and eventual deportation to Auschwitz. But while Frank wrote that in 1944, it could just as easily apply to numerous other Jewish communities going back to ancient times.

Jewish history has continuously taught us that we will never be fully accepted by the non-Jewish world. No amount of cleverly planned campaigns, money, or political influence can change that. Just ask the Jews of Roman Alexandria. Or thirteenth-century England. Or fifteenth-century Spain. Or 1930s Berlin. Or 1940s Baghdad. The details may differ, but the end result is always the same. And yet, as post-Holocaust Diaspora communities experienced perhaps the greatest levels of success and integration in Jewish history, we committed the sin of allowing ourselves to forget the lessons of our past. "We were," as Jewish-American writer Bari Weiss observed in 2020, "on a holiday from history."

One place to look for inspiration is in the ultra-Orthodox community. More than any other Diaspora community, they know they're different, and they don't care. In fact, they embrace their difference. And it works: In 2022, the London-based Institute for Jewish Policy Research estimated that ultra-Orthodox Jews, who then made up "one in seven of the world's Jewish population," would constitute "at least one in five" Jews by 2040. This is not to suggest that we all don black hats and spend six hours a day in a *beit midrash*. But the clear lesson from the ultra-Orthodox is that Jews thrive most when we unabashedly embrace the fact that we are not like anyone else.

Some Jewish thinkers have already begun articulating such an understanding of Jewish identity. As Horn explained to me, Jews don't fit into modern categories of religion, race, or nationality. Rather, she says, we "predate" them all. So what are we? According to Horn, Jews are a "joinable tribal group with a shared history, homeland and culture. Part of that shared history, homeland, and culture is a non-universalizing religion." But what seems on first inspection like incomprehensible jargon is, in fact, astonishingly simple once translated into Jewish lingo. "In Hebrew it's one word," Horn says. "*Am.* We're *Am Yisrael.*"

It may have occurred against our will, but history's tendency to remind Jews that we are eternal outsiders—especially at times of immense social and economic privilege—is far from happenstance. To accept this reality is not to give up. It is an embrace of Jewish destiny, the secret to our survival and thriving, and the key to keeping newly active members of our community engaged in the long run.

Whether we choose to capitalize on this opportunity is up to each and every one of us. But if we do, we'll go a long way in transforming this moment in Jewish history into not just a time of Jewish trauma, but one in which we helped secure the Jewish future.

11

Stop Overfocusing on Antisemitism

Kivi Franks

November 12, 2023: With an Israeli flag in my back pocket and my *kippa* tucked into my side pocket, I walked in Melbourne's central business district alongside the pro-Palestine march, a weekly occurrence since October 7. For miles, densely packed crowds lined the main streets. To be clear, I was there as an observer, not a supporter. I felt compelled to be there, to see it with my own eyes. I think my motivation to attend was because I refuse to be intimidated in my hometown. It was an act of quiet, personal resistance.

I usually get frustrated when Jewish people take offense at Palestinian flags. It's a flag representing a people, deal with it. And yet I felt offended, and threatened in the midst of thousands of Palestinian flags, in a crowd calling, "Intifada," "take out Zionist trash," and "from the River to the Sea." An

Kivi Franks is student of Commerce and Engineering at Monash University in Melbourne, Australia. He is involved in the Jewish community, holding roles such as College Captain at Leibler Yavneh College, Madrich and Rosh Chinuch at Bnei Akiva and Education Support at Leibler Yavneh College. Kivi worked in the Hasbara department of the Prime Minister's Office in Tel Aviv in the early months of the war, preparing Daily Briefings for English language media.

enormous gathering of people was collectively calling for the violent destruction of the Jewish homeland (*my* homeland) and the ethnic cleansing of its people (*my* people), whether or not they realized it. In moments like those, Israel feels less like the place of hi-tech, falafel, and cherry tomatoes, and more like the Jewish people's response to the Holocaust and all the massacres that came before.

I observed the type of people who attended. It seemed clear that a concerning proportion of attendees chose to be there out of sheer hatred for Jews and their land. (Months later, I was verbally assaulted as I walked past a pro-Palestinian protestor after the Sunday rally. He called me a "*kippa*-wearing f**got" and a "f**king ugly dog.") Many others were there with true humanistic intentions. Young parents brought kids in their strollers. They'd seen the rubble of Gaza on television, and that was enough.

Their protests are misguided, of course. No one had given them the memo that supporting barbaric, genocidal terrorists wasn't going to make life better for Palestinians. Given the constant drumbeat of anti-Israel media, one can understand why ordinary Australians might show up to those rallies. I assume they don't know that many organizations behind these protests are supporters of Hamas, Hezbollah, and the Iranian regime.

✱ ✱ ✱

The media—not just in Australia but around the English-speaking world—are frequently guilty of two different fallacies which combine to paint a distorted picture of the conflict. The obvious one is the oppressor-oppressed narrative in vogue today among progressive radicals but increasingly expressed in the mainstream liberal discourse, which leads many to overlook the massacres and gang rapes and mass kidnapping, and to advocate on behalf of genocidal terrorists.

The second is more common and subtle—namely, "equivocation" reporting. Exploring both sides is crucial for good journalism but, in the case of the Gaza war, it reflects a kind of obsession with presenting all sides as equally valid, to a degree unseen in other areas of coverage. Formulations like this are obvious: "October 7 was bad, but it's the Palestinian response to half a century of oppression in Gaza." It's more concealed in this kind of story: "Palestinian activists protest genocide in Gaza, Jewish leaders call out antisemitic rhetoric." Headlines you almost never see in mainstream media are the ones that read: "Jewish leaders reiterate justice of war in Gaza, to dismantle Hamas and to rescue hostages in wake of October 7 massacres."

In Melbourne, after a rally against antisemitism was crashed by pro-Palestinian protestors, one of Australia's major news channels reported violent "clashes" in the city, leading to numerous arrests. What they didn't mention was that the clashes were between police and pro-Palestinian protestors, and that every single arrest was among the latter. It was subtle and easy to miss that the authors and editors deliberately decided to spin the report as "two-sided," building an impression that both sides are equally guilty.

All of this media-driven distortion, problemaic as it is, creates an additional problem: It leads the Jewish community to focus intensely on antisemitism at the expense of arguably more important priorities such as learning about, visiting, and publicly supporting Israel on its own terms. To put it bluntly: We are allowing our enemies and their supporters to set the agenda of our communal life.

Media-driven Israel-bashing is a problem, but we don't help ourselves. There is a mistake being made too often by Jewish Zionist voices: When haters cry "genocide," we cry "antisemitism." You do not have to convince me that antisemitism is a serious issue. After October 7, global anti-Jewish hate has skyrocketed. And while they might not understand it, because it has never been explained to them, activists' obsession with Israel *is* antisemitic, because they apply a different set of standards to Israel, and when far greater human rights crises unfolded, they are silent. To make "Israel" and "Zionism" the central evil of our world is no different from making "Jews" the central evil a century ago.

But the average pro-Palestinian activist wouldn't understand that, and neither does the average onlooker.

When our representatives call opposition to Israel "antisemitic," often they are not wrong. But they contribute to the impression that criticizing Israel is antisemitic. This is an insult to the soldiers defending Israel, who do so with utter commitment to ethics and law. That message needs to be shared first and foremost. We need to help outsiders support Israel by speaking about our commitment to what is right.

Too often, calling out antisemitism comes at the expense of proud support for Israel, the IDF, and the need to bring home the hostages. Of course, both Jews and Gentiles have the right and responsibility to criticize fairly, but it must start with a fundamental message that Israel is good and that we are proud of our country.

Around the world, rally after rally in recent months has been centered around antisemitism, which is important to talk about. But it seems to me that increasingly, as it is scarier or less popular or more intimidating to support Israel, we take the easy route and cry antisemitism. But then everyone shows up with their Israeli flags. You can oppose Israel rallies, but no one can oppose a combatting antisemitism rally, right?

I worry that we are we're too ashamed to say we advocate for Israel and Zionism, and it's easier to resort to saying we are just fighting antisemitism. But what message does that send to outsiders? They'd be forgiven for coming to the conclusion that our only response to their accusation of genocide and war crimes is that it is antisemitic. There are millions of kind people who see suffering in Gaza and make the simple assessment that it is because of Israel; those people we can and must inform. We must explain to them how Palestinian suffering is the result of Hamas and that dismantling terrorism will improve Palestinian lives.

* * *

While many complain about all the non-Jews who have gone silent on anti-Zionism and antisemitism, I ask:

Where are all the Jews? We expect everyone else to support our country, but even if they are supportive behind closed doors, they will never admit it until we do—until Jewish institutions, famous Jews, and larger numbers of ordinary Jews get loud and proud about Israel. Until *you* have plastered your Zionism all over your identity, for all to see. It's easy to be proudly anti-antisemitism. We must make it easier for others to be proud Zionists by being prouder Zionists ourselves.

They bully us when we allow ourselves to be bullied—when we hide. They respect us when we are proud and outspoken, refusing to hide, when picking on us is less easy and less fun. Yes, we are victims of terrible crimes, but the Jewish way is the way of resilience—refusing to define ourselves by our oppression, and taking pride in our successes. The more we exude pride and strength, the better off we'll all be for it. Talk about antisemitism, but talk more about your love for Israel and for your Jewish history, traditions, and identity.

12

The Jewish Family Comes First

Tracy Frydberg

"Why do you care more about Israel than our family?"
my younger brother asked me after I made Aliyah
from Texas to Israel. My parents taught us that family was
the highest value. So it seemed misaligned for me to distance myself physically from those I loved most in order to
fulfill the Zionist dream. In the last nine years, I've never
managed to give him a compelling answer. In this current
period when loyalties and priorities have further crystalized, I think I'm getting closer.

It's never solely about the State of Israel—not my Zionist dream and not even the core purpose of this war. It's
about the family. The family is the nation, and the nation
is incubated in the home—whether Israel or Texas. This is
particularly clear in a period when we find ourselves in a
war being waged against the Jewish family and nation. As

Tracy Frydberg is the director of the Tisch Center for Jewish Dialogue at ANU–Museum of the Jewish People. Tracy served as a senior advisor to two of Israel's Ministers
of Diaspora Affairs and previously worked as an analyst on Israel-world Jewry relations
for the Reut Group. Previously she served two years in the IDF as a representative to the
Palestinian population in the West Bank. She holds an M.A. in Jewish Peoplehood from
the University of Haifa.

the core of Jewish community, when the family is weakened, so is our society.

The most urgent task, now and in the days to come—not only for me, but for the Jewish people at large—is to protect the family in the private sphere and the nation in the public sphere.

Understanding how to get through this period and bring about "the day after" requires understanding how the notion of "family," and the assault on it in October 7 and its aftermath, play out in distinct and intertwined ways for Israel and the Diaspora.

* * *

For Israel: On October 7, when Hamas terrorists broke the Gazan fence, they targeted the family: mothers and fathers, and their children. Animalistic cruelty was carried out within the intimate home.

When the IDF didn't show up, parents—like *Ha'aretz* journalist Amir Tibon—called their parents. It was Tibon's father, 62-year-old Noam Tibon, who knocked on his son's door, with a "Dad's here," rescuing his son and grandchildren.

Entire families were wiped out in the October 7 massacre. Entire families lost their homes, were split apart, and are still waiting for their loved ones held hostage in Gaza.

The Israeli war continues to play out against the family. More children have been orphaned since October 7 than all of Israel's wars combined. Day after day, pained parents look out at crowds through their exhausted, heartbroken eyes to demand that their children's values and dreams and bodies not be forgotten—mothers like Rachel Goldberg-Polin, who pled for the release of her 23-year-old son Hersh, held in Gaza, to anyone who would listen, before he was executed in captivity; or like Sarit Zussman, who lost her son, Ben, in battle, and now speaks across Israel, spreading her wish "that our story will have a happy ending, that *Am Yisrael Chai* forever—for ever and ever, until the end of the end, to be specific—and that we need to live up to the greatness of the moment, all of us."

In the war's aftermath, the Israeli family continues to be both uniquely targeted and uniquely heroic.

For the Diaspora: Outside Israel, the fight against the Jewish family began on October 8, when pro-Hamas "joy rallies" broke out across the western world.

This war targets not the physical body so much as the soul. It pounds on the Jewish family and its individual members' identity and status. Its strategic aim is to divide the Jewish people, between the Diaspora and the Homeland, the young and the old.

With little rehearsal, parents now guide their children on how to present in non-Jewish spaces. They are figuring out if there's a time to hide and another to show pride. Take my mother's JCC barre instructor, who at the start of the war asked her whether the mezuzah on her door made her family safe or vulnerable. They must manage generational divides over Israel, affecting who is at the family table and what is said. Then, once parents have offered direction, the children ultimately make their own decisions about how to engage with Israel, their Jewish community, and their larger surroundings.

Whether here or there, this period hits the global Jewish people in its most vulnerable touch points, returning the Jewish individual and collective back into our primordial role as members of a family—connected to past, future, and living Jews.

Perhaps, in the decades leading up to this crisis, we American Jews and Israelis started to forget what it felt like to be a part of this family.

* * *

The casing that encloses the family—that is, the home—is meant to serve its members. When the home, and the possessions and people that sit within it, begin to drive priorities away from the family unit and its members, the family is weakened.

This is where Hamas and its global allies found the Jewish people on October 7.

On October 6, as an outcome of Zionism's success, Israel was the focal point of both pride and divide in the Jewish world. "Jewish national sovereignty" had won out as the most compelling answer to the most central Jewish question, "What keeps us safe?"

Since the Holocaust and certainly after the Six Day War, Israel has driven the Jewish people's priorities. For several decades, this is what kept us safe and united. But in the years leading up to October 7, it began to prove problematic.

Over the years, American Jewry's focus on Israel and the institutions that supported it allowed the intimate American Jewish family to outsource identity and belonging to the State of Israel and its Zionist story. Jewish identity became something to be found on a Birthright trip, not at the family Shabbat table.

In more recent years, the government and politics of Israel have seemed increasingly to misalign with young American Jewry's values and sensibilities. But if Israel was at the center of their families' Jewish identity, then when the Jewish state disappointed American Jews, their own Jewish identity—including the older generations and frameworks supporting this identity—disappointed them as well. While American-Jewish "Israel education" compensated for this strain by encouraging "hugging and wrestling" with questions around Israel, hugging and wrestling with living and breathing Israelis was extremely rare.

For Israelis, of course, Israel was always at the center of their Jewish experience. The creation of the Jewish state and its army represented for them nothing less than the "end of Jewish history." This facilitated a rejection of their entire society's understanding of itself within the longer and larger Jewish narrative, and as such, with contemporary Diaspora Jews. To be a Jew was to be an Israeli, and to be an Israeli was either to reject the Diaspora or to ignore it. This was reinforced in the Israeli educational system, which encouraged a narrative of Jewish history going "from Tanach to Palmach"—that is, from the Bible to modern Israel. The curriculum left little space for the story of contemporary Jewish civilization beyond Israel's borders.

As a result, this rising generation of Israelis enjoys only minimal literacy about global Jewish peoplehood, let alone identity. And just like their American peers, they lack the deep relationships with global Jewry that come from interacting in shared spaces.

These dual realities have made it more difficult, yet more pressing, for the Jewish people both in and outside of Israel to work together for the betterment of the family in our generation's most dire hour as we, separately and together, ask again, "What keeps us safe?"

* * *

When the Jewish people do come together, we tell stories not of kings and queens, of great military prowess or treasures. We tell the story of family, which is meant to be, as it has always been, at the center. This is, in essence, the Tanach: a dialogue between parents and children who play out their relationships and tensions over generations. The archetypal Jewish story of Exodus is told from within the family home around the Passover Seder, led by its oldest and youngest participants. In this story, we are taught that not only Moses, but also his siblings Miriam and Aaron, brought the Israelites from slavery to freedom.

In our current story, it will also be the family leading us to the other side. Both within the intimacy of the family home and across the diverse vastness of the Jewish nation, the rising generation of "not quite children" but "not quite adults" is uniquely positioned to lead this joint work.

This requires that each young Jew choose to place the family unit as the central incubator of Jewish identity and belonging. We are in the critical decision-making years where we will determine what kind of family we will establish, what gifts we received from the previous generation that we aim to pass on to the next, what inherited traumas we might want to put to rest or evolve for our betterment. Let's build a new generation of heroic Jewish families.

Collectively, however, this means something else: placing the Jewish people as our highest of priorities—a people with a thriving Jewish nation-state, driven by its original Zionist mission to serve as a home for the Jewish people to come together. Placing the state in its proper context, at the service of the larger family, will allow our generation to build a healthier relationship with our home and with each other. It will empower us to make painful political sacrifices for the sake of bringing about a shared Jewish future.

* * *

Israeli educator and social activist Netanel Elinson wrote, "This war, this war of families, a war in which whole families pay the heaviest price, reminds me how important my family is. How much more and more our ties need to be strengthened. How much proportionality is needed, and how nothing is taken for granted."

Perhaps this is why the brother who thinks I love Israel more than I love him decided to spend this past summer of war together with me. Now a nineteen-year-old American college student, he spent five weeks sleeping on my couch in Israel. And after the initial hugging, there was also a lot of wrestling.

The reality is that we are meant to live close to the ones we love. If we can't, then we must be intentional about coming together to build and to nurture our relationship, hugging and wrestling whenever we have the chance. This is what builds the intimacy and trust naturally found in a home. In order to compensate for distance, both physical and ideological, young American Jews and Israelis must create shared spaces to drive our shared work.

Only together can our generation commit to protecting and to building our family, our nation.

13

We Are Israel's Greatest Generation

Avi Gamulka

The forces of courage within our midst have erupted in an inspirational manner," declared Israel's President Isaac Herzog in January 2024, in a letter marking the one hundredth day of war since October 7. "We saw how the 'TikTok Generation' emerged as a generation of historic strength, whose bravery will be etched in the annals of Israeli history. I met with the fighters and commanders, the leaders on the front—made of steel, eager to engage the enemy, with the oath of 'never again.'"

Herzog's words captured a sentiment felt all across Israel during the early months of the war: an intense admiration for Israel's younger generation, inevitably accompanied by a note of surprise. And in fact, young Jews, both in Israel and around the world, "stepped up" beyond anyone's expectations. In the process, they offered the hardest commodity to come by during those awful months: hope.

Avi Gamulka studies History and Geography at The Hebrew University of Jerusalem, and serves as an advisor to the president of the World Zionist Organization. He has previously served as a policy advisor for the director-general of the Prime Minister's Office, as spokesman for the minister of tourism, and as a *Foreign Affairs* correspondent and senior news anchor for GLZ—Israel's Army Radio.

Young people, of course, have been disparaged for thousands of years. Plato and Aristotle each took potshots at the youth, with their "decaying morals" and "wild notions." Yet, this being an ancient phenomenon has not made the criticism easier to swallow for Gen-Z. Herzog's "TikTok Generation" label captures the essence of it—we have stood accused of preferring "quiet quitting" to an honest day's work, as if growing up online somehow made us lazier and more entitled than those who came of age watching *Happy Days* and *Full House*.

For our generation, however, the problem was not just one of image, but of an objective sense of crisis that previous generations never faced. Ours is the first generation to experience the world as consistently getting worse. We're poorer than our parents, more depressed, more anxious, less likely to own homes, and enjoy less job security, all while being told stories by Baby Boomers about buying houses for seventeen dollars through hard work and determination. Even before we lived through the deadliest attack on Jews since the Holocaust, we had already dealt with unprecedented lockdowns courtesy of a deadly pandemic, and have watched with despair as temperatures rise, glaciers melt, and our only planet burns.

✳ ✳ ✳

In other words, the enemies of the Jewish people had every reason to believe that when mounting their horrific attack on October 7, they'd meet minimal resistance. They thought they'd meet a generation of Jews—in Israel, the U.S., and worldwide—who would collapse like a house of cards.

How wrong they were.

Within hours, and long before any official order had been given, hundreds of thousands of fighting-aged reservists had already reported for duty. Driving south and north independently from all over the country, some with no gear or weapons at all, they answered a call to save Jews from peril. They did not think twice before leaving their families and holiday tables. They thought of nothing other than what they could do to help.

The individual stories of heroism are almost too many to comprehend. There was Aner Shapira, 22, who was at the Nova music festival. When the attack began, he and his friends took cover in a small public shelter with no door. With terrorists closing in, he assured the more than twenty people in the shelter that if grenades were thrown into the tight enclosure, he'd catch them and throw them back out. Unarmed, he protected the small opening with his body, throwing back no fewer than seven grenades with his bare hands before one took his life. His courage and sacrifice bought invaluable time for those hiding inside.

There was Ben Shimoni, 31, who fled the Nova massacre and made it to safety, only to turn around and drive back twice more to try and save as many people as he could. Lt. Adar Ben Simon, 20, led dozens of young military cadets to safety at the Zikim training base, before leading a charge on the incoming wave of terrorists. Sgt. Matan Abergil, 19, saved the lives of six friends by jumping on a grenade that had been thrown into their armored personnel carrier.

Nor was this valor seen only on the battlefield. In the days, weeks, and months that followed, young Israelis stepped up anywhere they were needed: volunteering with refugees who had fled from all across the country, entertaining and educating children in hotels and makeshift trailer schools, picking crops from abandoned fields, renovating dilapidated bomb shelters, babysitting for families of reservists who had been called off to war.

The list goes on and on. For weeks, the most common hashtag on Israeli social media was *lo noflim midor tashach*, which translates loosely as "we're as great as the generation of '48"—just as selfless, brave, and values-driven as the pioneers and fighters who founded our country.

How did our generation go, in the blink of an eye, from being the "TikTok Generation" to worthy of comparison to The Greatest Generation?

The answer, I believe, is simple. In a word—Zionism. In three—*Zionism is hope.*

* * *

The near-perfect storm that hit us on October 7, 2023 struck during a time of acute economic struggle and after nearly a year of political crisis that tore our nation apart—which themselves followed years of stress and anxiety, climate crisis, the pandemic, and more. Ours was a generation in desperate need of hope, in need of a cause. October 7 suddenly restored the factory settings in our collective psyche, and together we remembered that Zionism *is* hope.

The early Zionist thinkers knew this well. In his foundational 1882 pamphlet *Auto-Emancipation*, Leon Pinsker was adamant that without purpose and drive, the Jewish nation would die. Jews, he wrote, "must not consent to play forever the hopeless role of the 'Wandering Jew.' It is a truly hopeless one, leading to despair.... we are bound by duty to devote all our remaining moral force to re-establishing ourselves as a living nation." Zionism, Pinsker believed, was a psychological tool to avoid despair. Rabbi Jonathan Sacks aptly called the Zionist project "the principled defeat of tragedy by the power of hope," and one need not look further than our national anthem—"Hatikvah" ("The Hope")—to know that building a strong, vibrant, independent, and flourishing Jewish state is, and always was, our two-thousand-year-old source of hope.

Within days of the assault, our generation discovered that we had found our cause—much like the founding generation of 1948, with its waves of young Zionists who reached the shores of Palestine and found a source of hope in the face of the brutal antisemitism of their time.

Two important steps lie before us. The first is to spread our message of hope as far and wide as possible—that Zionism is the answer. Enough with the angst and the social, economic, and political dread. Worried about the future? *Be the future.* Rebuild the homeland any way you can.

The second step, the true culmination, must be to embrace our role in leading that rebuild. We, the young Jews of Israel, the United States, and across the Diaspora, must fully internalize that we are the new Greatest Generation.

The leadership shown on the battlefield, on the homefront, on college campuses, at pro-Israel rallies, in synagogues and youth groups, must now be translated into leadership positions in the community as a whole. It is time to translate our fire into a seat at the table. For lack of a better expression, as Lin-Manuel Miranda put it, it's time for our generation to be in "The Room Where It Happens."

We've proven beyond doubt that we're capable, that we're necessary, and that we have the tools to envision a better tomorrow. Our time is now.

14

Say It Loud: Judaism *Is* Zionism

Rebecca Guzman

On the morning of October 7, 2023, my family and I slumped against the wall of a stairwell in the French Hill neighborhood of Jerusalem. We listened to sirens blaring, rockets soaring overhead, and the deep, far-off thuds as they fell to the ground or were intercepted midair. My brother and sister-in-law wore pensive expressions; they had been here, in this stairwell, before. But my parents and I, the New Yorkers, were afraid. "Misha," my mother whispered to her son, "is this serious?"

My brother shook his head and smiled. He did not want his young children to think that anything was wrong. But it was.

Less than seventy miles away, Hamas terrorists were setting houses on fire, slaughtering babies in their cribs, and sexually assaulting their mothers. They were kidnapping the people we still wait for today, devastating entire com-

---

Rebecca Guzman is a Straus Scholar at Stern College for Women, where she is currently studying Creative Writing. Her work has appeared in *Jewish Journal* and *The Jewish Press*, and she has received recognition from the National Council of Teachers of English and *The New York Times*. She lives in New York City.

munities before triumphantly reentering Gaza with their spoils. In the stairwell, we did not know this. All we knew about were the rockets.

Days later, as our plane hovered over Europe, I looked out the window and thought about the many decisions that had led us to Israel in the first place. In 1990, with the fall of the Soviet Union, my mother arrived in America from Belarus, after spending months crisscrossing through Europe. Ten years later, she met my father, another Belarusian immigrant. They married and built a house in Staten Island. And then, eleven years later, my brother flew to Israel for the second time in his life. As the president of Boston College's first pro-Israel student organization, he was to spend six weeks in Jerusalem's Old City before returning home to graduate from college and begin law school. It was a simple plan, one that did not take into account the power of the experience.

"Mom, something happened to me," read my brother's email. Huddled together in the kitchen, my parents read his words aloud, their faces shrouded in disbelief. The aspiring lawyer was now to become a rabbi instead, trading law school for the yeshiva. After a few years, my parents came around, forgoing their anti-theistic notions for a warm embrace of Orthodox Judaism, and my brother and his wife moved to Jerusalem.

It was a love for and commitment to Israel, and the discoveries my brother made there, that initially charted the course for us all. So, for as long as I can remember, my Judaism—and therefore my identity—has been tied to my Zionism.

✳ ✳ ✳

In the months that have passed since October 7, the strength of this tether has been tested. The connection between the Jewish people and the Land of Israel has been poked and prodded, investigated and researched by those who distort truth. "How deep is this connection?" they ask. "How old is it?" They seek to peel back the layers of history, to locate the exact, quantifiable moment when Jews first arrived in Israel and started to attract calamity. It is as though Hamas's terrorism—the goals of which they explicitly state in their charter—can be explained by the relationship between Jews and Israel. It must be that some inherent flaw in the Jewish people's self-determination, their statehood, their Zionism itself, has brought evil upon them.

Over the past generation, Western Jews have begun to pull at the threads that join them to Israel. It has become easy and even desirable to reject Zionism. Some Jews have sought to remove themselves from this narrative or to place themselves on the side of the apparent victors of October 7. "As a Jew…." they write, hiding behind screens as they condone terrorism, renounce Zionism, and forfeit—consciously or unconsciously—a core facet of their Jewish identity. On October 7, the day of the deadliest attack on Jews since the Holocaust, the pro-Palestine organization Jewish Voice for Peace (JVP) released a statement claiming that "the source of all this violence" was "Israeli apartheid and occupation." As quoted by the Anti-Defamation League (ADL), JVP activist Ariel Koren has said that Hamas's crimes are "consistent with Palestinians' right to resist.'" In January, *Jewish Currents* published a comic titled "Israel's Defense," in which IDF soldiers are depicted as brutalizing unclothed Gazan men while filming themselves. Above the head of one soldier, a speech bubble reads: "It's a blood libel to hit 'play' on our genocide TikToks!" Israeli flags poke out of destroyed buildings.

As defined by the ADL, Zionism is "the movement for self-determination and statehood for the Jewish people in their ancestral homeland, the Land of Israel." But somehow, to this particular group of Jews, Zionism is utterly separate from one's Jewishness. Jewish members of JVP, like Koren, can now block bridges while shouting for a ceasefire—a ceasefire does not include peace or an end to conflict—and calling for the United States government to stop sending aid to Israel as it defends itself. Jonathan Glazer can "refute" his Judaism on stage at the Oscars as he accepts the award for Best International Feature Film for *The Zone of Interest*—a film he made about Auschwitz, where approximately 1.1 million of his brethren were killed.

In its essence, Jews who reject Zionism are rejecting the premise that Jews should have a state where they can live without being persecuted. Perhaps it is possible to believe, in the comfort of one's San Francisco home or Camden flat, that the game has ended, and we can finally stop running. Centuries have passed since the Crusades and the Spanish Inquisition, and we are generations removed from the gas chambers and death camps of the Holocaust. Perhaps it is possible to believe that we do not need to be Zionists anymore.

But if Hamas's calculated acts of savagery on October 7, and the world's response since then, have proven anything, it is that the game is not over. Those who hate Israel do not, for the most part, exclude Jews from their hatred. Zionism is inherent to Jewish identity, and no amount of anti-Zionist Jews can change this truthful perception. On October 21, protestors at an anti-Israel rally in Rhode Island chanted "Hey hey, ho ho, the Yahudi [Jews] have got to go!" This is only one example of antisemitic sentiment expressed within the context of anti-Zionist activism, but it is emblematic of what is a much larger trend: The curtain between those who oppose Zionism and those who loathe Jews has grown precariously thin. Despite the common refrain trumpeted by social-media trolls and zealous protestors—that anti-Zionism is not antisemitism—it is difficult to see how calling for the eradication of the world's only Jewish state, or writing that the land must be "free" of Jews to allow for Palestinian sovereignty, is not antisemitic.

* * *

Throughout history, in every time of crisis, Jews have been forced to consider what we value, what we prioritize, and what challenges us. As Israel fights to defend itself against the terrorist group that seeks its destruction, and the subsequent destruction of the West, it is crucial to remember that this war is another in the long series of wars that has shaped

Jewish identity. Regardless of one's qualms with the Israeli government or disillusionment with Judaism itself, in order for the Jewish people to have a future in the Diaspora and in their historic homeland, Zionism must once again become intrinsic to Jewish identity. We must value ourselves, we must prioritize our statehood, and we must accept the challenge of defining our identity.

As the first-century sage Hillel once said, "If I am not for myself, who will be for me?" These words are ancient, but their message is timeless, as this is the question we face now. If the Jewish people do not identify as Zionists, then who will ensure that our state lives on? If we do not believe that we deserve a place to live and worship freely, to go dancing without never returning home again, to wake up on a holiday morning with our loved ones sleeping safely in their beds, then our future will not only be dark. It will be virtually impossible to ensure. And, as Hillel concluded—"If not now, when?"

15
The Amazing Tapestry of Our Identity

Sadie Hilf

I recently returned from my sixth Birthright trip as a staffer, and my second since October 7. It was a group of twenty-three North American Jews, ranging from 23 to 27 years old, mostly unaffiliated, many there only because it was their last opportunity to take advantage of the gift of a free trip before they aged out.

The trip ended with twenty-three raging Zionists. So, what happened over the course of those ten fateful days?

Jewish pride happened.

I was introduced to this line of thinking by the author Ben M. Freeman in his books *Jewish Pride* and *Reclaiming Our Story*. It should not have shocked me that the antidote to the profound anguish, disconnect, and confusion that characterize so many young Jews is Jewish pride. What's clear is that the Jewish pride that young Jews like myself desperately need is not of the old-fashioned Masada-Sho-

Sadie Hilf is a Campus Advisor at Hasbara Fellowships, and is concluding her Master's Degree studies in International Relations at Johns Hopkins SAIS, focusing on security and governance in the Middle East. She has worked with organizations such as New Zionist Congress, the Rimon Movement, Original Jewish Media, Tel Aviv Institute, Lost Tribe, and Taglit Birthright Israel.

ah-Sabra variety—the stereotypical story of Zionism that generations of young people have received: "Our last greats fell at Masada, we were forced into exile until the Holocaust happened to us, we were able to return home with the permission of outside forces, and now you too can be a strong, native-born Israeli."

It was a fitting story for its time. But let me tell you a different story for our challenges today.

* * *

As a child, I attended a school that advocated hands-on learning and had a robust arts education program. In first grade we learned to thread large plastic needles with yarn, and then to pass the yarn through large beads. Now, for a first grader, this was impressive. I took the bracelet home to my mother, but it was flimsy and did not take long to break.

As we grew older, we developed more skills. In fifth grade we learned how to weave fabric. We were able to pick out beautiful pieces of fabric to represent different aspects of our identity, and then worked for weeks to feed them through our small weaving machines until we had a square of fabric that was representative of our life story. This small piece of fabric was much more durable than our first-grade bracelets. Until very recently, this little life-tapestry was being used as a coaster in my childhood home.

What does this have to do with young Jews and their connection to Jewish history and Jewish knowledge? The bracelet I made in first grade is similar to the manner in which we approached Jewish history before October 7: a monolithic narrative thread clumsily shoved through important points in Jewish history in an attempt to create a linear story of the Jewish people. Like that bracelet, it was fragile. And on October 7, it broke.

What we need, now, more than ever, is a Jewish pride that is not based on a clever narrative thread being strung through beads of important points in Jewish history, but rather something more like what we made in fifth grade: a rich tapestry in which Jewish life is connected to its many different communal histories on all sides.

The good news is that the tapestry of Jewish life has been woven for centuries, and we are not starting from the beginning, but rather returning to this semi-abandoned project. The beautiful reds of the Persian diaspora are interwoven with the brilliant blues of the pre-state kibbutznikim, the indigo *techelet* of the Temple or the royal purple *argaman* of the Davidic kingdom. The emerald green of the Jews of the Iberian peninsula complement the sunshine yellows of the Beita Israel of Ethiopia. The dirt browns of the pogroms of Europe, Russia, and the Middle East, and the midnight blacks of the Shoah are there as well, but they are far outnumbered by the peacock pinks and purples of the Bene Israel diaspora in India and the complex oranges and greens from the Pale of Settlement.

Now, as we select the fabrics and threads to continue and expand the tapestry of the Jewish people, we must not forget that by weaving these diverse experiences together, we are all a part of the same fabric of the Jewish people.

And it is a heavy tapestry, not because horrible things have happened to us, but because of the richness of our history.

* * *

Where I believe the weight of the tapestry of the Jewish people fell on these Birthright participants was not at the Kotel, or in the clubs of Rothschild Boulevard in Tel Aviv. Rather, it was in the more mundane aspects of the trip.

It was no longer the story of the rebels of Masada that galvanized these young Jews to take pride in their identity; actually, they found the rebels of Masada quite reckless. It was working the land on a farm in the Arava desert, it was meeting their Israeli peers who had hopes, dreams, and fears just like them, it was singing songs of peace around a bonfire, it was driving through the Judean desert and watching young people herd flocks of sheep just like our ancestors did thousands of years ago. It was not the distant and dramatic historical tragedy that connected these young people, but rather their discovery that they were a part of a long, valued, storied tradition much larger and more complex than they had ever imagined.

It is not up to me to define how this generation chooses to weave ourselves into this tapestry. It is the young Jews like those on my most recent Birthright trip, the young people who showed up in droves to volunteer after October 7, the brave IDF soldiers and reservists who gave literal blood, sweat, and tears, and in too many cases their lives. It is these people doing incredibly brave, daring, and necessary work to preserve the Jewish nation that will define what our addition to the tapestry looks like.

Interestingly, one sentiment that many of my recent Birthright participants shared was that they felt as though they had been forgotten or overlooked by the Jewish community—and that by coming to Israel, they had found a place for their Jewishness. They had realized that their birthright was not just Judaism, or Israel, or the trip which bears the name, but rather the totality of the rich tapestry of Jewish peoplehood and the pride they could have in it.

This is not solely a post-October 7 phenomenon, of course. Birthright's immense survey data on Jewish identity post-trip shows that this impact is quite profound. But the fervor of my more recent Birthright participants in threading themselves into the tapestry of Jewish peoplehood has been remarkable.

* * *

All of this raises three important questions: First, why did it take these young people until the third decade of their lives to connect to Jewish life? Second, why was it only upon their journey to Israel that the connection began? Finally, is there anything we can learn from this, to begin the process at an earlier age?

To address the first question: Many of these participants had received their "bracelet" of Jewish history as a young person, and it had broken due to years of antisemitism, educational neglect, and institutional indifference.

Before October 7, entry into Jewish spaces in the Diaspora required having that bracelet still intact, and without a sustained connection to the Jewish community, there was no way for most young Jews to enter.

Why was this connection formed only upon a journey to Israel? Because for the first time in most of their lives, my participants were in the presence of a diverse Jewish majority, which allowed these young people to feel safe to explore their own identity, to ask hard questions about themselves and others, and to find others like them.

And how can we begin weaving these forgotten threads into the Jewish tapestry well before a "once in a lifetime" trip to Israel? The answer lies in beginning to show the tapestry of Jewish life to these young people at a much earlier age: the Persian diaspora, the reality of pre-state Israel, the Torah, the lives of Jews in various European empires, the tragedies faced by every Jewish community around the world—and the beauty of our resilience. This information should be presented in a way that is relatable, accessible, and intriguing, owning up to the less than perfect parts of our history while proudly showing off our contributions to the tapestry, and demonstrating to others how they can do the same.

We bring in these forgotten threads with Jewish pride. And with Jewish pride, we can ensure that every young Jew can weave a rich, diverse, and deeply rewarding Jewish tapestry of their own.

16

Zionism of the Heart

Bella Ingber

I did not choose to be a Zionist. Being a Zionist is my birthright. It is part of my DNA, inextricable from my Jewish identity.

To fight this truth would be like putting my shoes on the wrong feet; it may be functional, but it's uncomfortable, and eventually I will stumble and realize that something is not right—an experience we Jews have endured throughout our history of exile, and a discomfort that we are confronting now throughout the Western world.

I was nine years old when I first visited Israel, buzzing with excitement and curiosity. My family was celebrating my cousin's Bar Mitzvah, and were staying in Jerusalem; from our hotel, we had a perfect view of the Old City. We toured extensively from 6:00 a.m. until 11:00 p.m. for eight days, and by the end of the trip, it felt as though we had seen the country in its entirety.

Bella Ingber is majoring in Psychology at New York University. As the president of Students Supporting Israel at NYU, Bella has been interviewed in national news outlets including Fox News, MSNBC, NewsNation, and ABC news, and spoke at a press conference in Washington D.C. ahead of the December 2023 House Education Committee's hearing on campus antisemitism, that featured the presidents of Harvard, University of Pennsylvania, and MIT. She is also the opinion editor for the *NYU Review*, a centrist alternative to NYU's *Washington Square News*.

I will never forget that trip, and I will most definitely never forget my family's tour guide, Aviad. Early in our tour, Aviad took us to the Judean desert. As we exited the van and walked towards a lookout, we were surrounded by a beautiful, barren, sand-colored mountain vista. My family gathered around Aviad as he pulled a tattered leather book from his pocket, its spine barely holding the pages in place.

"So, where are we?" he asked as he flipped through the heavily worded pages with confidence and comfort. Holding the page he had turned to, he read us an excerpt from the Hebrew Bible, and pronounced: "This is the only guide you need here."

For the rest of the week, as I jumped off of the rock formations into the freshwater springs at Ein Gedi, Aviad used his book to point out where King David hid from King Saul. As we waded through the tunnels of the City of David, Aviad's book explained to us how King Hezekiah utilized these same tunnels to ensure the Jews of Jerusalem had access to water amid the imminent threat of siege from the Assyrian army. It seemed that no matter where I walked, where I looked, where I stood, the Jewish historical presence—both physical and spiritual—was there, irrefutable, supported by centuries of evidence, all compiled into a leather-bound book that fit in Aviad's pocket.

✳ ✳ ✳

Zionism is ancient—there has been an uninterrupted

Jewish presence in Israel for thousands of years. Zionism is the right of Jews to self-determination in their ancestral homeland.

Since the horrors of October 7, my peers at NYU have tried to turn the word "Zionist" into an epithet that excludes and delegitimizes my voice from conversations surrounding the Israel-Hamas war and the broader Israeli-Palestinian conflict. My campus has become a breeding ground for hostilities towards "Zionists"—a codeword for "Jews," since the overwhelming majority of Jews support the right of Jewish settlement in their ancestral homeland. Following Hamas's attack on October 7, as I've stood strong in demonstrating support for Israel and the Jewish right to defend ourselves, I have been referred to as a "pink-washer," "genocide supporter," "new-Brooklyner," "apartheid supporter," and "bigot." I have been told that "anti-Zionism *isn't* antisemitism," and have been compared to the Nazis, a comparison that generates particular disgust for me given that my grandparents survived the Holocaust.

At NYU, a place that purports to value "diversity, equity, and inclusion," Zionists—and therefore the great majority of Jews—are intentionally excluded. Among the self-proclaimed inclusive groups that claim to preach radical acceptance and believe themselves to be bastions of inclusivity, I am no longer welcome. A girl in my sorority consistently contacted me after October 7, not to share her concern for the hostages or even to decry the senseless loss of life—both Israeli and Palestinian—but to share her distorted narrative that Israel is solely to blame for Hamas's barbaric attack because it is an oppressor. My sorority "sister" refused to acknowledge Israel's right to exist, or even to condemn Hamas. Most notably, she told me to "separate my identity from the conflict," that I and other "Israel sympathizers" acted like "self-righteous politicians with their identities tied to controversial issues." I responded, "My identity *is* tied to this controversial issue."

In the Spring of 2024, I spent Passover with my family in Tel Aviv. For the first time in six months, I didn't have to worry about whether I could safely wear my Star of David necklace in public, without fear of leering, menacing eyes or physical danger. For the first time in six months, I was finally able to breathe. I felt at home. Unless you're in Israel or have visited in the past, this feeling of security, in the middle of a war no less, is indescribable.

* * *

Zionism tends to manifest itself in two forms: Zionism of the mind and Zionism of the heart. The first approach focuses on the practical need for there to be a Jewish state, as an answer to economic, social, and political discrimination and degradations experienced by Jews for two thousand years in the Diaspora. The second construct, however, is a need for a homeland driven by emotion, culture, history—by feelings that are rooted in the Jewish people's connection to this piece of land. When in the Diaspora, Jews focus on sustaining the State of Israel, supporting it through political and pragmatic solutions in order to ensure a Jewish homeland. As a Jew in the Diaspora, I'm often guilty of solely using this approach, and find myself defending my Jewish identity from the throngs of antisemites on NYU's campus by resorting solely to an understanding of political history and political need.

But during my most recent trip over Passover, the safety and sense of belonging I felt when walking through the ancient cobblestoned streets of Jerusalem, biking on the beach in Tel Aviv where people from all religious, ethnic, and cultural backgrounds basked in the sun, riding the bus with my Star of David sitting unobscured on my chest, the weight that lifted from my shoulders reaffirmed for me the connection I had felt on that first family trip to Israel. It reaffirmed for me the importance of Zionism of the heart, a powerful defense that I will bring back with me to campus in the fall.

Zionism is not just the idea that Jews deserve a state of their own—anyone can claim that. It is, rather, the belief that Jews deserve the right to self-determination in our *ancestral homeland*, in Israel, an irrefutable truth based on our history.

The Jewish connection to Israel is not political; Israel is not the product of colonialism or of American imperialism. It is, instead, the manifestation of a two-thousand year longing of an indigenous people to return home. This fact is, and should be, the cornerstone of the defense of our Jewish, and, by default, our *Zionist* identities on campus.

To Jewish students who keep finding themselves forced

to jump through political hoops constructed by their peers in order to justify Israel's existence, gaslit into believing that the history of the Jews in Israel began in 1948, and frustrated when that approach is consistently "undermined" and deemed "invalid," I have a book that I think might help. It's called the Bible. Happy reading.

17

It's Time for the Grown-Ups to Step Aside

Noah Katz

For my generation, the last five years have been anything but normal. From March 2020, when the pandemic began to dominate our lives, to the Hamas invasion of Israel on October 7, 2023, to the shocking yet (for anyone who's been paying attention) totally unsurprising massive uptick in antisemitism in all parts of society and particularly in Western higher education—the kids are, quite simply, not alright.

All of these events, along with a more general sense of *WTF is going on?*, are deeply interconnected. They have created a younger generation of Jews very different from those who came before. The future of Jewish survival must begin with Jewish institutions understanding who this new generation is. Who we are.

Yes, each generation is different from the one before it.

Noah Katz is an award-winning media host with strong experience in Jewish advocacy, who is passionate about diverse involvement in political spaces. As well as being the youngest chairperson of a Jewish Community in the world in 2023/24 (Lancaster and Lakes), Noah is the Chair of the Board of Deputies' Under 35 Assembly and sits on the Board's executive. Outside of the Jewish community, Noah serves on the board of the National Union of Students (NUS), holds a B.A. in Cultural Studies (with a focus on the Jewish Diaspora) from Lancaster University and, in Fall 2024, is set to earn an M.Sc. in Human Resource Management from Lancaster University Management School.

But there is something different about Gen-Z and Gen-Alpha. The gap began before COVID, but was severely exacerbated by the social isolation of lockdowns.

Now, before you start telling me that the pandemic was awful for all of us—it was particularly awful for those under eighteen. I was lucky enough to have started university pre-lockdown. I had already moved out of home and lived, briefly, as an independent adult.

Being a teenager was different before COVID. You went to school, had fun with friends, and, most importantly, you were able to make mistakes in a safe environment without the risk of grown-up repercussions.

For my generation, the world ended in March 2020. Kids were stuck at home on Zoom, worrying about their grandparents dying, instead of socializing, having fun, being silly—being children. Young children were locked away from any meaningful social interaction. Some regressed.

Then, a few months into the apocalypse, the narrative of race in Western society shifted. For those of us in our late teens or university years, this was the second of what would become a succession of tectonic shifts in a relatively short period.

The Black Lives Matter movement didn't start in 2020, but George Floyd's dying words of "I can't breathe" and the video of his brutal murder spread around the world. While people were suffocating in hospital beds, a police officer named Derek Chauvin needlessly took the life of a father of five. Debates around race, racism, and the systemically oppressive nature of how society is constructed broke through to the mainstream, and with it came a new language.

This novel language, which emphasizes social justice and a desire for what the Spanish philosopher José Ortega y Gasset called a "hyperdemocratized" society, seemed to become a *lingua franca* for younger people. It's lazy to blame BLM, DEI, or whatever three-letter acronym you're annoyed at today for the ills of the Jewish people in 2024. The fact is that while young people may speak a different language from those who have come before us—we also *think* differently. To make matters worse, during our formative years, spaces for young people to engage in nuanced dialogue were killed by COVID. As a result, we didn't have the space to disagree, and to explore that disagreement, safely.

The de-nuanced *novel lingua franca* manifests now in four different ways.

First: Due to lockdowns, perhaps, we show collective compassion more forthrightly than our elders. We spent two and a half years having to mask up, not for ourselves but to protect others. We could hear what people were saying but couldn't see them saying it. The facial expressions weren't there. We were forced to trust people based on what they said, but not how they expressed it. Not only did COVID kill our ability to engage in dialogue, but expression became inhibited. You never knew if you were reading people right. It was strange, but we knew it was necessary in order, eventually, to bring the End of Days to an end.

Second: As a result, perhaps, of this heightened sensitivity to collective compassion, younger people today also have a greater understanding of the intricacies of intersectionality. This is why we're able to move away from the reticence of our elders to lean into the discomfort that can come from efforts to build bridges with other minoritized groups.

Third: we will not accept diktats from legacy organizations representing the perspective of older generations. *Nothing about us without us* springs to mind. We're demanding seats at the table, not on the sidelines, to help form the world we want to see.

Finally: my generation has broadly grown up in a world where Israel's existence is non-negotiable. It's just a fact. Unlike our grandparents, who witnessed its establishment, or their children, who saw it teetering on the brink, we see Israel as a hard truth, like any of the many countries that came into existence after World War II. With that comes new conversations around the meaning of Zionism.

Am I a Zionist? That depends on how one defines Zionism. If Zionism is just believing in the right for Jewish self-determination in our ancestral homeland—then, sure as shit, I'm a Zionist. I know that Israel is one of the only places in the world where it is safe for Jews to exist as Jews.

If, however, Zionism means that one isn't allowed to criticize or actively campaign against the Israeli government or establishment—then, no, I'm not a Zionist.

* * *

From my perch the other side of the Atlantic, in the United Kingdom, I can see that a deep schism has erupted in American Jewry, between Zionist and anti-Zionist Jews. Is this schism simply the wider trend of a divided world playing out in our communities? It seems our *mishpocha* across the pond are preoccupied with internal division, but strangely unwilling to rip off the Band-Aid (as Americans put it) and do the surgery necessary to repair. I know our people's history, and I know that it shows exactly why we need Israel.

So, why are more young people becoming inclined to move away from "traditional" Zionist ideals? In short, we see what those ideals have been bastardized into.

It doesn't make me any less of a Zionist to want a free Palestine; I would argue it makes me more of a Zionist. I protested the judicial "reforms" in 2023 *because* I love Israel and I am a Zionist. I called for a ceasefire in the war in Gaza *because* I'm a Zionist.

My Zionism, especially after October 7, puts peace a the center. It posits that for the homeland of the Jewish people to thrive and to flourish, we have to give to get. We have to work empathetically with people we don't understand, rather than just expecting them magically to understand us. Working only with "moderates" who agree with us on the easy things is a lazy approach; instead we need to be brave and have the difficult conversations. Think of it like theater: In order for the director's vision to emerge, participants have to suspend their disbelief. Their disbelief that the "other" side is wrong or evil or lying just because they're the other side—for humanity to succeed, the basic humanity of all people must be in the fore of all conversations.

So, why am I a Zionist? I'm a Zionist because I believe in hope. Hope for our people, and hope for all peoples who live between the river and the sea. I yearn for a free Palestine and a secure Israel. Yes, I'm an idealist. But aren't all ideologies based in idealism?

* * *

Back home, I see the British Jewish community balanced on the edge of a precipice, and I'll be damned if my community falls into the abyss. If we want to "ensure the future of the Jewish people," as legacy organizations never stop telling their donors, can we please do away with this willing misrepresentation of the challenge we face? It's not about ensuring the future so much as accepting the changing face of the present. This begins with understanding just how different my generation is, and when necessary, *stepping aside to let us take the lead.*

That is to say: I'm not a leader of tomorrow, I'm a leader of today.

It may be controversial to say the quiet part out loud: Most legacy Jewish organizations are conservative in nature. Institutions inherently dislike change; all the more so large, century-old institutions.

This conservatism can often lead to the silencing of new voices precisely because their leaders don't want to see their own power diminished. I'm not pointing out this problem because I want that power, but the failure is a problem because we are seeing so many Jewish organizations flounder with youth engagement. While every new generation is different from the one before it, ours has gone through so many upheavals in so short a time—from lockdowns to social justice, from the crisis of Israel's democracy to October 7 and the explosion of antisemitism—that we have emerged fundamentally different from even the millennials who are just a bit older than us. Legacy institutions, led largely by Gen-Xers and Boomers, can barely understand what we're saying.

Since the end of 2022, one of the main things legacy Jewish organizations were talking about was "Jewish unity." Seeing the reactions of the Israeli population to Netanyahu's fascist-adjacent cabinet rippling like a tidal wave across the Diaspora, organizations thought that the lack of unity was *the* issue that we, as a people, must address.

Over the summer of 2023, I attended, in Jerusalem, the launch of an initiative built to foster "Jewnity" as I sometimes like to call it. Led by the World Jewish Congress, one of the legacy organizations who are getting youth engagement right with their NextGen programming, we were brought together at Nefesh B'Nefesh Headquarters to hear from President Isaac Herzog, who opened the afternoon of lively discussion between emerging and established Diaspora leaders and top voices in Israeli civil society, with a message of enthusiasm to take into our work: Stop talking, he urged us, and start doing.

In the weeks after the October 7, some commentators said that the problem of Jewish unity was solved because of the pain we shared. I disagreed. To me, it all seemed temporary, like a family coming together at a shiva. You don't want to upset things, but the feelings are still there. Grief rarely fundamentally changes feelings. It often just covers them up.

What I'm saying, in other words, is that we have to *find an answer*, not just talk about it endlessly. We can't just ignore it but have to do it, and *really* do it, soon. These Jewnity conversations aren't for nothing; they're really important. However, the crucial thing that seems to be missing from them so often is the willingness to actually change. Yes, we sit at roundtables and get to know each other for two hours at a time, but for those two hours to be worth it, the power balance has got to shift. A good leader leads from the middle, not the front. A good leader knows when it's time to step back and let others do the talking.

It is time to let the new generation take the lead.

One example of a legacy organization doing just that is the Board of Deputies of British Jews. At the beginning of 2024, I was elected as the first Chair of the Board's Under 35 Assembly, a body designed to ensure that the over 260-year-old organization remains fit for the future by listening to the people who'll be leading it in ten, fifteen, or twenty years' time.

Like a shark, we have to keep swimming or risk death. Jewish communities the world over, please, let your young speak for themselves. Let us change your tired systems for the better. We're not a threat. We have the same deep-rooted love for our people as you do. So, give us your resources, give us your endorsement to create something better. Let us not just shake your stale systems up, but allow us to flip them on their heads and reverse all the barriers to participation. I'm fed up of working around the antiquated system; I want to make the system work for me.

Just like my criticism of Israel isn't based in baseless hate, this too is based in so much love. I love the Jewish people, so I want to change us for the better.

18

A New Golden Age of American Jewry?

Shabbos Kestenbaum

When Rabbi Yosef Yitzchak Schneerson, the sixth Lubavitcher Rebbe, fled Nazi persecution and arrived in the United States, he was warned of the spiritual wasteland that engulfed Western civilization. America, he was told, would be unlike the shtetls of yesteryear, intolerant of the flourishing of traditional Jewish life.

"*America iz nisht andersh*," he replied. America is no different. Judaism could be sustained there.

Whether he knew it or not, Schneerson's prophetic insistence was rooted in historical precedent. In his 1790 letter to the Newport, Rhode Island Jewish community—numbering roughly twenty-five families, then the largest in the new United States—President George Washington promised that things would be different. The newborn United States would give "to bigotry no sanction, to persecution no assistance."

Indeed, for the next two centuries, American Jewry set

Shabbos Kestenbaum is a student activist and the lead plaintiff against Harvard University, alleging pervasive and systemic antisemitism. He is a regular contributor on national media, has testified in front of the United States Congress multiple times, and lectures internationally on Jewish communal issues.

out to prove Washington right. By building institutions of Jewish life from the shores of New York to the plains of Texas, participating in all avenues of societal life such as politics and entertainment, and contributing thousands of lives to defend it, America was, by all quantitative metrics, a vehicle that enabled the flourishing of Jewish life.

My story of American antisemitism, therefore, is as deeply painful as it is personal.

As my last name Kestenbaum suggests, my family's origins are traced to Germany. My great-great-grandfather, Rabbi Yosef Breuer, was the leading German Orthodox rabbi and a respected figure within German society. Rabbi Breuer's youngest daughter, my great-great aunt, vividly recalls praying from the Book of Psalms while the Nazi Gestapo arrested her father and their historic Breuer Synagogue in Frankfurt completely burned to the ground, all on the night of Kristallnacht in November 1938.

But Kristallnacht did not begin with book burnings or broken windows. It did not begin with destroyed synagogues or expulsions. Kristallnacht began with a pernicious ideology that swept across German society.

Kristallnacht began with the acceptance, normalization, and celebration, of Jew-hatred.

* * *

The treatment of Jewish Americans on college campuses across this country is nothing short of a national emergency. It is blatantly antisemitic, it is frighteningly discriminatory, and yes, it is how a Kristallnacht begins.

As a Jewish student at Harvard University, I say these words from two years of personal experiences with a racial ideology, championed by Harvard, that views Jews as an annoyance at best, with pervasive bigotry at worst, and overall suffers from a stunning deficiency of moral clarity.

In my time at Harvard, swastikas were drawn in undergraduate dorms, a Jewish student was spat on, an Israeli student was asked to leave class because her nationality made classmates "uncomfortable," another Israeli was assaulted at the business school, a staff member taunted me with a machete and challenged me to debate the Jewish involvement in the 9/11 terrorist attacks, our hostage posters were defaced almost daily, and professors published antisemitic cartoons without facing discipline. Harvard students illegally set up encampments all over campus, demanded Harvard divest all moneys from the Jewish state, cheered thunderously when they replaced the American flag overlooking Harvard with that of Palestine, screamed about globalizing the Intifada, drew pictures of Harvard's Jewish president with horns and a tail, screamed at all hours of the day that "Palestine will be Arab," established their own rule of law on campus, and followed us Jews on our way to class—all while Harvard either refused to acknowledge these incidents publicly, failed to address them for months, or did not discipline the perpetrators.

While many of us tried for years to reform Harvard internally, our efforts all proved futile. Harvard stubbornly insisted that everything was fine; they were both unable and unwilling to confront the problem.

While we are not facing a Kristallnacht yet, the hour is close to midnight. These unchecked acts of antisemitism—and more so, the normalization of antisemitism—are deeply concerning and dangerous. Indeed, the deteriorating situation at Harvard and across the country caused *The Atlantic* to feature a crucial question prominently on their front cover: "Is the Golden Age of American Jewry Ending?"

My answer is simple: not without a fight.

* * *

In January 2024, I had the privilege of filing a historic lawsuit in federal court against Harvard University, alleging a culture of pervasive, systemic, and ingrained antisemitism.

While the choice to resort to such a drastic and public move was difficult, the lawsuit is much bigger than Harvard. It signals that Jewry is willing to defend itself. Thus, I remain proud of our fight, a fight that allows us to express our values openly.

These values have been instilled from the very community and family I grew up in. My mother would often play the great Israeli singer Naomi Shemer in the car; I even remember the day Zionist icon Arik Einstein died. With five siblings currently living in Israel, including two who have served in the Israel Defense Forces, Zionism has been an ingrained aspect of my religious identity. The inherent spiritual attachment to my ancestral homeland spurred me to engage with the Land of Israel itself, including studying in Jerusalem for two years.

To see this critical aspect of my religious expression denigrated in such hostile, vicious ways, at a supposed bastion of intellectual vitality and academic rigor, was deeply distressing at best, and illegal at worst. The lawsuit not only holds universities accountable for their horrific treatment of their Jewish students, but also draws an inherent connection between Zionism and Judaism.

In it, I detail decades of normalized antisemitism, both subliminal and explicit at one of America's most important institutions.

Fortunately, I wasn't alone in fighting back.

* * *

Since October 7, a monumental shift in the story of American Jewry has taken place. More than 150 Jewish students from across the United States have filed similar lawsuits against their universities which detail damning reports of unvarnished, naked Jew-hatred.

These lawsuits, marking a watershed moment in American Jewish history, represent much more than the claims we argue in court. For the first time, Jewish students are unabashedly stating their values under oath and holding their institutions accountable.

We will force our universities to recognize the fundamental truth—that they have allowed their libraries and study halls, classrooms and quads, to be infected by anti-Zionist poison that places the Jew as settler colonial and Israel as an outpost of imperialism. The truth, however, is simple to us students: "Zionism" is not a dirty word. The State of Israel is a beacon of democracy in an unstable region. The Jewish people are not expendable.

With these avalanches of legal filings, there is much to be proud of. In the last year, countless young Jews have taken up the fight for Zionism and the Jewish people. They are testifying eloquently in the United States Congress, they are speaking powerfully to the national media, and their bravery is inspiring millions across the world to see that *od lo avda tikvatenu*, our hope is not yet lost.

Ultimately, while October 7 unleashed unparalleled antisemitism in the United States, it has awakened a new spirit within young, Jewish Americans. This next generation is full of impassioned Zionists who recognize Israel's promise and the necessity of keeping it strong. I can confidently assure those who are worried about college encampments and hostility towards Israel, those who are worried that the Golden Age is ending, and those worried that support for Zionism and her ideals is eroding—to merely look at the Jewish students speaking out. The future is in good hands.

We are proud Zionists, proud Jews, and proud Americans.

We are no longer afraid to fight for the Jewish State, its people, and its ideals, be it in the classrooms, on the quad, or in the courtroom.

Why? Because *America iz nisht andersh*.

The Golden Age of American Jewry is not ending, it's simply evolving into a new phase—one in which young

Jewish Americans will not simply be responding to the current reality, but creating a new future, filled with determined and passionate American Zionists.

19

Seek Justice, the Jewish Way

Issy Lyons

The value of justice is at the core of Jewish thought, embedded in Jewish tradition, and central to our national identity. While external factors may change, Jewish justice remains unchanged, in contrast to the Western perception of justice which plays to trend. The future of the Jewish people and the State of Israel rests on our ability to stand by our moral beliefs and to continue to strive for what we know is right.

In Deuteronomy we are taught, "Justice, justice shall you pursue." (Deuteronomy 16:20) The repetition of the word "justice" is a deliberate reminder of the centrality of justice to Judaism. However, we are by no means the only tradition to cry out for justice. Martin Luther King, Jr. famously said, "We shall overcome because the arc of the moral universe is long, but it bends toward justice." These words have brought hope to many, offering a belief that justice is inevitable.

Issy Lyons made Aliyah from Hong Kong in 2020 to serve as a combat soldier in an IDF field intelligence unit. She is currently a student in the Columbia University and Tel Aviv University Dual Degree B.A. program. Her writing has appeared in the *Jerusalem Post* and the Hartman Institute's *Sources: A Journal of Jewish Ideas*.

While King's concept is beautifully optimistic, it makes the arc of the moral universe into the subject, with justice as the final object. According to this theory, justice is not necessarily a set of laws and principles one should follow, but rather an abstract end goal. In the modern world, King's words have been taken to mean that while the moral arc is long, even if it doesn't always look that way, freedom, equality, and justice are nonetheless an inevitable reality.

To the Jewish view, such an approach is both misleading and wrong. A more realistic look at the moral universe in King's time would be more like a wave rather than an arc. He was speaking in 1968, only twenty-three years after World War II, one of the darkest times in human history, one that was by no means morally better than any time before it. If nothing else, it would have been legitimate to question what, other than idealism, was his basis to theorize that the arc could possibly be a curve programmed to bend towards better times at all.

King's pursuit of justice, including the concept of protest, has been taken even further and has in many ways been the groundwork for the social justice warriors of today. This interpretation has now been taken as an excuse for many clearly unjust events, such as the looting, riots, and general violence in the name of justice during the 2020 Black Lives Matter protests. Today the conception is largely based on current trends, in which activists prioritize movements that give them immediate gratification rather than focusing on more productive methods of creating real change. If King preached patience (the arc is "long"), today people are insisting on "bending the arc" right now.

* * *

If we are to believe that the arc bends towards justice, how could one begin to explain the events of October 7 and the world's reaction to it? Terrorism is on the rise, with calls for genocide and Intifada in the name of "justice" becoming commonplace. The mass slaughter of Jews, and the assertion that it was justified, are proof that *the world is no more just than ever before.*

So-called "social justice warriors" have attempted to redefine justice. They have molded the concept into a new form to fit the current trend and as a justification for their own hateful agendas. The world we currently live in is objectively unjust, with more bloodshed, cruelty through the use of instruments of war, and general violence, than nearly any other time in history. Only when justice is constantly redefined, rather than based on concrete rules and moral facts, can history be read as tending towards justice.

The Jewish people, however, don't understand the moral universe to be an arc, or justice to be inevitable. We don't play to trends. The mandate that we seek justice was written into our law thousands of years ago and continues to be our guiding principle. Justice depends entirely on our efforts—and if we do not fight for it, it will not happen by itself. Our task, therefore, is to hold the line and actively strive for justice.

While many in Western society see the moral universe

as an arc bending to justice, for us justice is a path to a truly moral universe. Long before the Torah explicitly calls for it, justice is written into our story. In the first chapter of Genesis, we read that "God said 'let there be light,' and there was light," which clearly does not refer to physical light, as the sun had yet to be created. Instead, this light refers to truth and justice. From this point on, justice takes an imperative role in Jewish life, practice, and beliefs; it is not an eventual outcome, but a driving force in our lives. We know that achieving a "moral universe" can be done only through continually seeking it: "Justice, justice *you shall pursue*."

In fact, in Judaism at its core, there is no arc. Justice is, as it has always been, one straight line that defines our ideal of a moral universe. Of course, we do not always act in a moral and just way. On the contrary, the point of a call for justice is that we do make mistakes and spend our entire lives attempting to return as closely to that *derech*, or straight path. While there have been new interpretations of our ancient wisdom, that path remains the same path that \ was set forth in our texts and is embedded into every aspect of our religion.

This is true even on the most tragic day of the Jewish year, Tisha B'Av, when we fast and mourn the destruction of both of our holy temples, the expulsion of the Jews during the Spanish Inquisition, and many other tragedies that occurred throughout history. We refer to the day as a *moed*, a holiday, and do not say Tachanun, the prayer of penitence traditionally said on mourning days. This is because, while the day is objectively sad, we also learn from our survival through all this hardship that ultimately we need to correct our path and focus on dedicating ourselves to creating a better future. This very much summarizes the Jewish mindset: We use our darkest moments as points of reflection in order to refocus toward a more just and brighter future.

Further, the Hebrew word for justice itself, *tzedek*, indicates the centrality of this concept to our daily lives. "Tzedek" is also the core of the words for charity (*tzedaka*), and for the righteous person (*tzadik*). There is no greater honor in our tradition than to be called a "tzadik." From a young age, we are reminded that being charitable and righteous are two of the most important aspects of being Jewish. The shared root for the two words illustrates how essential seeking out justice is for the Jewish people. This is what has kept us alive as a people and thriving for thousands of years.

Another word for righteous in our tradition is *yashar*, which literally means "straight." Perhaps the most influential rabbinic work of moral philosophy of the early-modern period was called *Mesilat Yesharim*, or the "Path of the Just." It was written in Amsterdam by Rabbi Moshe Chaim Luzzatto in 1740, at a time when Enlightenment ideas were spreading across Western Europe, and Jews were increasingly coming under their influence. This work served as a clarion call for Jews to remember their own conception of justice and to cling to it through every aspect of their lives.

* * *

Finally, the Jewish concept of justice is the exact opposite of the modern-day activist's search for immediate gratification. Jewish justice is largely based on following our laws and commandments. Tzedek is also defined as the straightforward pursuit of laws and moral truth. This is specifically seen during the Ten Days of Atonement, from Rosh Hashana to Yom Kippur, when we pray for mercy to soften the "hammer of justice." By this definition, justice and mercy are two opposing factors, meaning that the Jewish pursuit of a higher moral universe has little room for immediate gratification. Rather, it is focused on our understanding of right and wrong despite the current trend.

For these reasons David Ben-Gurion reinforced the belief that "The State of Israel and the people of Israel are to be a light unto nations." The phrase "light unto nations," originally taken from the words of the biblical Isaiah, can be understood in the context of the earlier passage from Genesis. Our light is the light of the first day of Creation. It stems from our pursuit of justice and is the essence of both our past and continued survival.

The secret to the survival of the Jewish people and the strength of the State of Israel is therefore straightforward. As we have done for thousands of years, we need to continue to look to the Torah and to strive to follow the values and morals that we know are right, following our "straight line of justice" and hoping that the "moral arc" of the rest of the world eventually reaches us. We can't afford to listen to the loudest voices or to tally popular votes. To us, justice is already defined and written into our way of life and our pursuit of the moral universe.

It is up to us, in the face of the injustices around us, to continue to stay on our path. We need to remember who we are and where we are going, but the path is a straight one.

20

Overcome Victimhood

Naftali Oppenheimer

The Western world has come to appreciate, more or less, the evil created by colonialism. This is, of course, a good thing. But it has also unleashed a torrent of identity ideology aimed at supporting anyone belonging to a demographic that suffered oppression in the past: women, people of color, LGBTQ+, immigrants, the poor, and more. The tenets of this ideology form the progressive worldview— one that contains the promise of a new world and a new morality, in which there is nothing more moral than standing courageously with those who are perceived as having suffered injustice in the past.

But what about someone like me: white, male, middle-class? It would seem that no matter what I do, no matter what sacrifices I may make for the oppressed Other, I will always be implicated in the historic injustices committed by people who look like me.

Naftali Oppenheimer is founder and co-director of Teva Ivri–Bar Kaima, a Jewish-Israeli environmental movement, and of the Hebrew Beit Midrash in Jerusalem. He is a social entrepreneur in the fields of Israeli Judaism, environment, and community, and a lecturer, project manager, and consultant for organizations in values implementation. He studies and teaches Philosophy, Bible, and Kabbalah, graduated with honors from the Open University with a degree in Social Sciences, and is completing a Master's Degree in Public Policy at the Hebrew University. He lives in Jerusalem.

This belief system spells the demise of enlightened humanism.

Humanism will die in such a world, because the unique individual has ceased to be the focus of a free society. For centuries, humanism promoted the individual who thinks, who chooses, who takes responsibility—the individual who has a name and a face, whose fate is not predetermined by gender or the color of one's skin.

Instead, today we see the rise of a movement that does not recognize names or faces, but sees only group identity. Everyone is reduced to an item in a category. In this world, I will never become more or less than a white male—another guilty party, born in original sin, one I did not commit and therefore can never atone for.

Of course, it is not only the white male who will forever be just an item in a category. So too will the presumed victims of injustice. Each member of their category—women, people of color, immigrants, LGBTQ+, and so on—will also be bound by the collective history of their own group.

At the end of the day, no individual will have a place in this new world.

And so, we come to a crossroad. One path leads to societal abyss. The other to a repaired world. To true Tikkun Olam.

If we take the first path, that of the new morality of collectives and categories and the demise of humanism, then—in order not to be left behind—I will need some kind of card to play, to demonstrate my own categorical victimhood. And I should also demonstrate a communal narrative of profound and prolonged structural oppression to go with it.

It turns out I actually have such a card, and a pretty compelling one at that: I am a Jew.

* * *

By any historical measure, Jews are the most oppressed population in history. There is not a single crime or atrocity that hasn't been committed against us. Slavery, rape, murder, defamation, and the killing of children. Pogroms, murderous mobs, death marches, ghettoes, expulsions, forced marches, and killing by every possible means. Thousands of years of institutionalized discrimination including prohibitions against buying land, against education, against employment, obligations to mark their clothing to humiliate them, prohibitions against self-defense. Powers great and small have taken out their wrath on the Jews since the Egyptian empire 3,500 years ago, via the Assyrians, Babylonians, Persians, Greeks, Romans, Christians, Muslims—and so many in the modern period.

So, there it is! We Jews really do have a place in this new world. We are not privileged. We are the greatest of all victims. We aren't just oppressed; we are the *ultimate oppressed people.*

Except for one problem. This new world leads to an abyss in which only those wounds that remain open and bleeding are worthy of attention, where there is only a masochistic incentive to be among those with open wounds.

The more I still suffer from past oppression, the more attention I will receive.

But most victims don't want to be victims; they aren't masochists. Do we as Jews really want to be categorized as inherently oppressed so that the hypocritical mob will love us? A healthy society, one of true Tikkun Olam, offers a cure rather than preserving the malady. We dream of a healthy society, one that fights against those who do harm, and helps those who are harmed.

Why is it that Jews are not accepted into the ranks of the oppressed? Why do the arbiters of oppression-status, those in charge of distinguishing oppressors from oppressed, show favor to a criminal with the correct skin color, but ignore the slaughter of Jews dancing at a music festival? Why do the same people who automatically believe a woman who testifies that a man touched her inappropriately second-guess a Jewish woman who is raped in her own home in front of her children? The common answer, that it's because of "antisemitism," is too easy.

Those who are injured and then heal, whether physically or societally, know exactly how much pain they have endured. But they also know that the people with the greatest responsibility for that healing are the injured people themselves. Of course we need to hold those who do the harm to account, to do everything we can to punish them and prevent further injury. But one who has *overcome injustice* has the greatest motivation to help others who have been harmed. Those who have healed themselves don't spend time feeling sorry for those who scratch at their wounds again and again so that they may stay in the hospital. They looks for partners in courage—other injured people who want to get better, ready to work hard to take themselves out of the pit they have been thrown into.

Why are Jews who have been harmed not given support? Why are Jews blamed when others are harmed, even if the Jews are the ones offering support? The reason is that Jews signify, more than anything else, those who, despite having been the victims of injustice, refuse to be oppressed.

Our very existence shatters the central thesis of the new progressive world.

* * *

Jews believe that we will always rise from the ashes. That the day will come when we redeem ourselves in a world of wolves and lambs. Jews are prepared to be partners in courage, without victimhood, without free passes. The Zionist movement did exactly this, rising from the furnaces of the Holocaust to establish a strong and prosperous nation, in the process bringing the Jews to full membership in the United Nations. Within half a century, a nation of refugees—who escaped the decrees of the Muslim world, who survived the Holocaust in Europe, who escaped the Iron Curtain of the Soviet Union—became free people in the State of Israel. People who add honor to humanity.

Similarly, the Jews of the Diaspora were also victims who, within only a few decades, rebuilt their communities for all the world to admire. This is especially the case of the

Jews of the United States, many of whom arrived as penniless, oppressed refugees, who then turned themselves into a powerful force in the struggle for freedom and democracy.

What kind of victims can these Jews possibly be, some may ask, if they don't stay victims into the next generation? If they *defy* the structures of historical oppression? Again and again, Jews prove over and over that the fundamental assumption of the progressive worldview is false, that the individual and free choice are the keys to rehabilitation.

In the eyes of the arbiters of oppression-status, however, those arrogant Jews refuse to be victims or to pass on their victimhood to the next generation. They are so arrogant that they dare to build a network of charitable organizations around the world, dedicating their time and philanthropy to an astonishing degree. How is it possible that a victim can also be an agent of bettering the world? Both oppressed and also a force of healing?

Our history proves that it doesn't matter how harsh reality is, or how much you are despised and thwarted—it is possible to recover. Our past is indeed unchangeable, but our destiny is expressed in the choices we make for the future. Everyone has a genuine right to be optimistic and to make themselves proud. Everyone has been blessed with gifts, some pleasant and others less so, that are tools for living in this world. And that basket of gifts begins with the image of God in every person. To be a Jew is to believe that it doesn't matter who you are, what color you were born, or what education you received. The choice to improve your life, to be a good person who pursues justice, is in your hands only.

* * *

The Children of Israel, the Hebrews who were enslaved in Egypt, could have chosen the position of victimhood. According to tradition, many actually did—and stayed behind in Egypt. But those who chose to overcome their oppression experienced an exodus to freedom under the leadership of Moses, and with them went many other slaves who were freed. The exodus was a matter of choice, not race.

For this reason, in every generation it has been possible to join the Jewish people. To convert in Hebrew is *l'hitgayer*, which means to turn oneself into a *ger* or a refugee. The meaning of converting to Judaism is to choose to join the community of refugees who choose to leave behind their victimhood. The aspiration of the Jewish people is to be neither slaves nor masters, neither oppressed nor oppressor, but freed slaves who forever maintain the ability to see the world from both perspectives. Thus we remind ourselves continually that we were once slaves in Egypt and are now free. In every generation, Jews free themselves from Egypt. In every generation we continue the historic covenant with the Creator of a Better World.

The Bible commands us not to despise Egypt, even though they murdered our children in the waters of the Nile, because not all Egyptians were evil; some were the righteous among the Gentiles. Not all Germans were Nazis. Not all Palestinians are Hamas. Not every white male is a colonialist. Both the weak and the strong are human beings, each of whom has the freedom to choose whether to pursue freedom and prosperity or to be stuck in the past. I alone am responsible for my choice whether to protect the Other or to close my eyes and ignore his or her suffering. And another open secret: Not all Jews are good people either. This is perhaps the greatest appeal of Judaism—we are always internally in conflict. That's a good thing. Because the world is always changing, one always has to respond, and different people make different choices, for good or bad.

I am a Jew—part of a tradition of morality and responsibility, of revolution but also of modesty and hope. I am a Jew not because of my DNA, but because my parents taught me that I am part of a heritage of exodus from the dark and into the light. And every human being may choose to walk in the light with me, Jew or non-Jew—we are all humans created in the image of God. Everyone is free.

In every generation, we must see ourselves as if we have been brought out of Egypt, and it will happen if we believe that morality is in our individual choices and responsibility, not in any external definitions. To be a humanist is a choice, and I choose it precisely because I am a Jew, because I believe in humankind.

21

Never Let Others Define Us

Fayga Tziporah Pinczower

Just one month after the Hamas assault of October 7, I joined college students from across the United States for a three-day conference in Washington, D.C., sponsored by a Jewish non-profit organization. We were there to learn about how best to advocate for a strong U.S.-Israel alliance.

As a first-year student at Yeshiva University, I considered myself fortunate that I had only heard, but not directly experienced, the vicious anti-Jewish intimidation and violence plaguing so many college campuses. My fellow attendees spoke of fists thrown, Jewish off-campus "retreats" (read: Jews fleeing campus till the mob settles down), and overwhelming hypocrisy as institutions that had prided themselves on "safe spaces" and "trigger warnings" now endorsed marches calling for the death of my people.

What startled me most was a phrase, repeated throughout the program like a drumbeat, uncomfortably new to my ears but so natural to those of my peers: "Jewish identity."

Some participants spoke of "burying their Jewish

Fayga Tziporah Pinczower is a Straus Scholar at Stern College of Yeshiva University. Her writings have appeared in the *Wall Street Journal* and the *Jewish Journal*.

identity," feeling it was a liability, while others talked about "discovering their Jewish identity" for the first time. Still others wondered whether being Jewish ought to factor into their identity at all. As one female Ivy-Leaguer put it, "My identity mattered more to the haters than it ever did to me. If I'm going to be hated for being Jewish, I may as well find out what it means." Since then, she and I have become Facetime *chavrusas*—study partners, delving into Jewish texts each Thursday morning as we explore that very question through the prism of our people's canonical writings. We agreed not to let others define our sense of self. We would return to the original sources, even if they were three thousand years old and couldn't be found on TikTok.

* * *

Since the first chapters of the Torah were written millennia ago, Jews have been asked, like the biblical Adam: *ayeka*—"Where are you?" Defining ourselves through our covenantal relationship to God, as the Hebrew Bible depicts, continues through the generations. Abraham responded, *hineni*—"Here am I"—no fewer than three times when called upon to abandon all he had known and to sacrifice his own son and his promised future nation. Abraham's faith through this most challenging of tests signified the fidelity to commandedness felt by Jews ever since.

Moses, too, had his "Here am I" moment, at the Burning Bush. Though a hesitant and stuttering individual lacking the "leadership skill set" that some of our most treasured institutions charge the equivalent of a house downpayment for, Moses nevertheless found within himself the tenacity to level demands on the tyrant of the unfree world.

A thousand years later, Queen Esther harkened to that same covenantal commitment, without a female empowerment squad, knowing that if she remained silent, "deliverance will arrive for the Jews from someplace else" but she and her family would be wiped out, because Jewish history has no bystanders—only timeless heroines and mortal men.

Although originally derelict in his duty, Jonah, too, assumed responsibility for the endangered lives of his fellow sailors onboard as well as an entire sinning city, even when the role of "national savior" seemed a fate worse than death. In declaring *ivri anochi*—"I am a Hebrew"—his assertion echoed through the ages, challenging the Hebrew present within each Godly-gifted soul to actualize himself or herself.

In other words, the modern term "identity" hardly captures the depth offered by three thousand years of Jewish texts and tradition.

That's why I suggest we Jews replace empty buzzwords like "indigenous" with *ivri*, or "Hebrew," which reminds us of our forefather Abraham who dared to stand "across the river" while the rest of the world failed to see Truth; who deliberated with God to save fellow humans but ultimately accepted His will; who tirelessly spread knowledge of God and divine moral principles to mankind.

Similarly I refuse to replace *yisrael*, or Israel, with "minority" when that name was hard-won by Jacob after fiercely struggling with both man and God. I refuse to discard *yehudi*—which means both "Jew" and "Judean"—for "oppressed," when the word reminds me that Mordechai, the *ish yehudi*, the Judean man, refused to bow to evil and understood that our miraculous existence depended on spiritual fortitude; and I refuse to abandon the *mamlechet kohanim v'goy kadosh*—the "kingdom of priests and a holy nation"—for "privilege," when the former bonds me to sacred covenantal dignity and responsibility.

When we allow others to define us, we relinquish our true Jewish essence and settle for a distortion dictated by others. We so easily will allow the continuation of the slow march recently described in Dara Horn's summary of David Nirenberg's *Anti-Judaism*, in the February 15, 2024 issue of *The Atlantic*:

> If piety was a given society's ideal, Jews were impious blasphemers; if secularism was the ideal, Jews were backward pietists. If capitalism was evil, Jews were capitalists; if communism was evil, Jews were communists. If nationalism was glorified, Jews were rootless cosmopolitans; if nationalism was vilified, Jews were chauvinistic nationalists. "Anti-Judaism" thus becomes a righteous fight to promote justice.

By adorning ourselves with causes and concepts invented by others, we're left culturally impoverished and spiritually lost. Like a battered woman, we've fled from shelter to shelter, relying on the good graces of our provisional host, convinced that if we only contribute more to the cause and stand out less, we may secure a temporary haven.

* * *

Of course, not all exterior definitions have been bad. Judaism made immeasurable contributions to the American and, more broadly, Western founding, where the term "Jew" has fared fairly well. In their introduction to the 2019 book *Proclaim Liberty Throughout the Land*, Meir Y. Soloveichik, et al., make the case that

> the Hebraic worldview, which runs deeper than language and cultural conversation, articulates a vision of human life that is redemptive, endowed with sacred meaning, and which seeks to combine righteousness and freedom. It is this worldview that has contributed to the American moral language of liberty.

Indeed, it is our biblical declaration emblazoned on the Liberty Bell, and no coincidence that almost every inaugural address includes biblical reference.

Yes, Judaism has found a haven in Western ideology. But let's not mistake one for the other. Anchoring Judaism to popular ideologies is simultaneously delegitimizing and self-defeating.

Abraham Lincoln called the Americans the "almost chosen people," for while Westernism and Judaism share common values, there are crucial distinctions highlighted most starkly by *halacha*—Jewish law. We Westerners prize meritocracy, yet a Yisrael or Levi can never become a Kohen. We value rationality, yet you'll catch me swaying with a palm branch come autumn. Sometimes Torah and halacha offend our modern sensitivities; but they are the beams supporting our lofty ideals. Civilized societies claim fealty to basic values, but without pragmatic and ultra-precise guidelines, values may be wielded to bolster both piety and perversion. Look no further than the current Israel-Hamas conflict for proof that "value for human life" may simultaneously promote and protest war. Values are vague and easily corrupted unless grounded in divine (and sometimes demanding) directives. Being "chosen" means we answer to the Chooser.

Jews may find hints of home underpinning Western tradition, but we mustn't forget Elijah's question to the ancient Israelites, "How long will you go back and forth between two different ideas?" Ultimately, Judaism and any ideology, even Westernism, are not synonymous. Judaism demands complete allegiance to God, because "Jew" is not an abstraction—it's a mission. And like Queen Esther in the palace or Jonah aboard a sinking ship, we too are asked, "Where have you come from? What is your country, and of what people are you?"

What will we answer?

If "Jew" is our true identity, it cannot be defined either

in opposition or in complement to something else. We must define it independently. If October 7 crystalized whom we stand with and whom against, our post-October 7 pledge is to discover *who we are when we stand alone.*

Rebbe Nachman of Breslov, the eighteenth-century Hassidic master, told the tale of a prince who suddenly decides he's a turkey. Unbridled by reality, the prince disrobes, crawls under the table, and commences his turkey-existence. Despite countless pleas, medical expenses, and novel incentives, the prince remains convinced of his animal identity.

Finally, as in all Jewish tales, the Sage arrives. He similarly disrobes and joins the prince under the table. Perturbed, the prince asks the Sage why he's acting this way. "I'm also a turkey," replies the Sage.

Nodding, the prince accepts this explanation, and the two sit together for some time. Hours pass before the Sage asks for a shirt. "Turkeys don't wear shirts," protests the prince.

"Why not?" retorts the Sage. "What makes you think a turkey can't wear a shirt?" Stumped, the prince acquiesces.

Next, the Sage requests proper human food, claiming that any smart turkey would want the tastiest dishes. The prince agrees.

The parable ends with the prince dressed in regal garb and restored to his royal seat, seemingly cured. But I wonder, does the prince believe himself to be a human prince or simply a brilliant, human-like turkey? Is he yet another estranged Jew, merely acting part of the tribe to dissuade the odd Sage and to gain social acceptance, or merely indifferent to the significance of his actions? Or maybe he simply prefers turkey to prince because, after all, turkeys don't need to study, work, or train to be the next ruler. No one expects a turkey to be better than it already is. Relinquishing our unique responsibilities for another identity may be easier—but we'd be selling ourselves short and doing the world a grave disservice.

That's why I'll never substitute my divine names, like *ivri, yehudi, yisrael* and *mamlechet kohanim v'goy kadosh* for any token titles. Had I distilled my "Jewish identity" prior to the conference in Washington, I could have cogently articulated that *gene, creed,* and *deed* bind to form Jewish identity. I could have explained that every member of the 0.2 percent of humans born to Jewish mothers is immutably Jewish regardless of practice, passion, or belief. But Judaism isn't composed of genetics alone.

To be a Jew, as outlined by Maimonides, is to believe in the existence of God, His unity, incorporeality, and eternity; to be a Jew is to commit to worshipping Him alone, to trust that He communicates through prophecy, and to commit to the veracity of Moses; to believe in the divinity and immutability of the Torah, God's omniscience and providence, reward and retribution, the ultimate redemption and resurrection of the dead.

Consequently, it's only reasonable to heed His will, as outlined in biblical and rabbinic law. Colloquially, Jews refer to God as *Hashem*—literally, "the Name." Indeed, remembering His name allows us to know our own.

In the meantime, my *chavrusa* and I will continue to

ask, to learn, and to implement—refusing to settle for a Judaism appropriated by the terms of others. I invite you to join us, not just on Thursdays, but every day. Hopefully, as we witness our miraculous existence, like a bush ablaze but never consumed, and ask "Who am I?" we will be brave enough to hear the answer and to harken to its call.

22

Israeli and Proud at Columbia

Maya Platek

There's a certain heaviness about being Israeli. It's understanding the weight of war as a child, but never being allowed to be the victim. It's learning how to mourn and carry on through devastating loss, despite the world refusing to allow you the chance to grieve. It's growing unattached and tough to traumas that my friends could never imagine. It's learning how to be resilient because you have no choice.

I've always known this heaviness.

It's learning to lie about where you're from when abroad at age 6, to avoid being physically attacked. It's having your passport spat on at 14, by an immigration officer

Maya Platek was born in Israel and raised in Tokyo, Japan. She is a senior at Columbia University studying Economics, Political Science, and History. Maya is the current Student Body President of her undergraduate college and a former board member of Columbia's Students Supporting Israel chapter. Maya served in the IDF Spokesperson Unit where she worked in the International Social Media Department as Head Content Writer. At college, she started a petition that acquired nearly 80,000 signatures calling for the dismissal of Professor Joseph Massad after he referred to Hamas's October 7 attack as "awesome." Maya has written for the *New York Post* and appeared on CNN, NBC, FOX, BBC, and in the *Wall Street Journal,* about her advocacy and the rise of antisemitism on campus.

who wishes that you'd "burn in hell" simply for existing. It's being told at 16, by someone you looked up to, that you and your country won't exist when you're 30. It's always being made to be the villain of another person's story, without ever having the opportunity to share yours.

Though I loved Israel, my family, and my country, growing up in the Diaspora I sometimes wondered—wished for—an identity that was a little less heavy to hold up. Would it be easier if I had been from somewhere else? Would sharing my nationality with others limit my opportunity to make friends? Would my nationality jeopardize my grades and future?

At times, it became clear that the answer was Yes: My life would be simpler if I were not Israeli.

As I watch my identity turn into a slur, I can see that many members of the Jewish community have felt the weight of the word "Zionist." When I hear it, I imagine it feels a lot like how "Jew!" sounded for centuries: something meant to be hidden and ashamed of.

My generation—and honestly, the generation before me—has co-opted it to mean "colonizer." I have been forced to engage in staunch debate with my peers about this, even before this current bout of war—specifically about whether I have a right to exist. Throughout my life, I have been asked time and time again, "Well, you're not a Zionist, right?" And I know that many of them are thinking that since I am a Zionist, I should not have the privilege to be sitting in the same classroom as them.

From chanting "resistance by any means"—which is

a call for violence and terrorism against an entire population—to physically attacking my Jewish classmates, to
comparing us to animals, the majority of my classmates
have made it clear that they're anti-Zionist.

Even though many have redefined it to mean "white
supremacist," Zionism is simply the belief that Israel has a
right to exist. Zionism is the notion that Jews, who by exile
were forced to integrate to a myriad of lands where they
were treated as foreigners, have the right to self-determination and statehood in their ancestral, indigenous homeland—the Land of Israel. As an Israeli, it is a core tenet of
my identity and nationality.

One can be critical of Israel's government and policies
(and many Israelis are), but often criticism of the Israeli government and the ideology of Zionism serves as a convenient
scapegoat for the hatred that runs deep around the world.
When the rhetoric turns to "I wish Hitler was still here," or
someone in my class emphasizes how my being murdered by
a terrorist would be a form of justice, I realize that being
Israeli means being viewed as subhuman.

Long before Israel was reborn, Jews were blamed for
the bad things that happened to them. As a result, many
chose to hide or distance themselves from their Jewish
identities, often even converting to another religion—none
of which helped when the Nazis took over Europe.

It devastates me to write this, but at times, I can see the
parallels in the current international Jewish community. As
Jews were once blamed for being the cause of antisemitism,
Israel has been made to be the cause—by non-Jews and

anti-Zionist Jews alike. Since October 7, I've had one anti-Zionist Jew after another tell me that Israel's existence—and its refusal to cave to the demands of its destruction—is the reason that they're being discriminated against in the Diaspora. As a result, just as Jews once distanced themselves from their tribe in a hopeful effort to protect themselves, they have distanced themselves from Israel.

The reckoning we have seen in the world in the last year proves that it won't save them. Whether one looks at Hamas's original charter, the Houthis' official slogan, or the Hitler-sympathetic rhetoric that has permeated protest movements in the West—sooner or later, they'll view us as one and the same.

***

Ironically, the antisemitism Israelis often experience gets blatantly ignored by the rest of the Jewish world. While Jews are the majority in Israel, we are a very small minority in our neighborhood of the Middle East, facing antisemitism and hatred that exceeds those of previous generations, perhaps comparable only to the Nazi era.

When Hamas terrorists embarked on their attack on October 7, to kill, kidnap, and rape civilians, they believed that they were "on their way to paradise." Just murdering us wasn't enough: They butchered our bodies so we would face death in the most painful way imaginable because in their world, destroying Israelis is salvation. From terror attack to terror attack—which now my classmates celebrate and call for with cries of "Intifada"—it seems a non-negligible number of people would kill Israelis if they could. It has been so normalized, and morally justified, that the world is accepting this as a legitimate viewpoint, even in seemingly reputable institutions like Ivy League universities, the UN, and the ICC.

The shattering of the common collective of Jewish identity—which sees Zionism as a critical component of our tribal identity—risks taking us all back to darker times, as it legitimizes false narratives in the same vein as *Protocols of the Elders of Zion* and other antisemitic narratives of the past. The antisemitic tropes of the Nazis are now alive at our universities. Professor after professor, administrator after administrator, and student after student at Columbia have made clear that in their minds it is entirely legitimate to express the antisemitic notion that Jews are money- and power-hungry.

Antisemitism has increased to its greatest apex since the Nazi era because this very hatred has united the supposedly liberal progressive movement with radical fundamentalist Islamists, whose values contradict everything these progressives supposedly stand for. The Supreme Leader of Iran, Ali Khamenei, sends his regards to protesting U.S. college students on X (Twitter), while murdering college students in Iran for protesting religious persecution.

For our generation to survive this, Zionist and non-Zionist Jews must stand united.

* * *

As I witness this period of rampant antisemitism, something my ancestors understood so well, I understand that my life would not be better if I had been born to another country. Growing up in the Diaspora, encountering and engaging with people from every perspective—every aspect of my identity was vilified, politicized, and ostracized. Every argument I have made, regardless of the topic, has been casually dismissed because of my Israeli nationality. Even in college, I have been told by well-meaning professors to hide my nationality as it might put me in danger. As I lose friend after friend, as I lose potential mentor after mentor, I sadly realize how right they were.

But how can I hide who I am?

I am Israeli. I didn't choose it, but if I had the opportunity to choose—I would never choose anything else.

How can I choose to hide something I have no reason to apologize for? How can I choose to lie about a country I love so much? How can I apologize for being the very realization of the dream that my ancestors had for thousands of years—where they suffered, again and again, and built themselves up piece by piece, just in the hope that one day their descendants would safely return to our homeland?

And like our ancestors beforehand, I have learned that being Israeli is learning to love through every challenge. To choose to fight in the name of love in the face of the hatred the world shows you.

In Israel, when people protest, it is not out of the hatred I have witnessed citizens of many other countries succumbing to—it is out of love. In protests, Israelis carry and wear the Israeli flag because we, as a people, unconditionally love our country and what it represents. It is not perfect, but it is home, and even though we as Israelis born in the twenty-first century have always known Israel, we carry the weight of the generations before us and understand what it means not to have this home.

It's knowing that even if you don't get along with someone, when it matters and something goes wrong—Israelis always have each other's back. We are one of the only people in the world who truly understands that we are stronger together.

Being Israeli is grieving every single loss as if they were your family.

Being Israeli is giving back a thousand terrorists just for one of our own, because we don't leave each other behind.

Being Israeli is being seventy-five years old and volunteering to fight Hamas terrorists as they invade a town and burn the people inside it alive.

Being Israeli is crying tears of joy when one of ours returns home, as if they were your son or daughter who had been held hostage.

Being Israeli is choosing to run directly to Israel when it is in flames, instead of away—no matter how daunting and dangerous it is.

Israel is not perfect, but Israel is the home that we regained and will never, ever lose again. I am honored to have the privilege of carrying this weight.

* * *

The Jewish world stands divided: between those hoping that they'll ride out this wave of antisemitism and distancing from Israel, and those who have chosen not to cower and instead to stand tall, even in the face of the world's hatred. But it doesn't matter which you are. Whether the narrative is that Jews are money-hungry or power-hungry, Zionist or not, it's still that Jews are money- and power-hungry. Whether it's just Israelis or Zionists being depicted as animals on posters, they're still the Nazi-era tropes that were once used to exterminate one-third of our people.

The overwhelming hatred dominating the media and newspapers is tough to withstand: but that's exactly why you have to hold on.

On October 7, we collectively felt shock, we mourned, we were shattered—but most of the world didn't feel that with us. Some of them, your coworkers, your classmates, celebrated it. Others have found ways to dehumanize what happened to us on that day, as if our lives are some sort of game.

Even if you've never lived in Israel or visited, as a Jew, the antisemites are conflating you with us; that's why they choose to protest at synagogues or in Jewish neighborhoods.

Israel is not your problem. The antisemite haters are. In fact, Israel is the only thing that stands in the way of repeating the tragedies that have plagued the Jewish people for centuries. For the first time we, the Jewish people, are protecting our fellow Jewish people from our enemies. And we are doing it together with millions of Muslim and Christian Arabs, Druze, and other fellow citizens. When the antisemites come after you (and one day, whether it's in a decade or in a century, they will), don't bend before their lies. Stand tall.

You are an honorary Israeli—and it shouldn't be something you're ashamed of. It should be a badge of honor.

And I am honored to be carrying the weight of being Jewish, and Israeli, with all of you.

23

Judaism Will Always Need Israel

Elana Rabishaw

One of my favorite aspects of my work as a con-gregational rabbi is teaching an eighteen-week Introduction to Judaism course. The students are always diverse in their knowledge and experience. The class varies in age from eighteen-year-olds to people well into their eighties. Some want to choose Judaism, some are life-long learners, and others are about to begin their own families and want to learn more than what they were taught as children in religious school.

As the daughter and niece of rabbis, I knew my job would come with its fair share of surprises, yet nothing could quite prepare me for the sheer eclecticism that even one day of this course would bring. As Forrest Gump might say, each week of this course is like a box of chocolates: You

Rabbi Elana Rabishaw works at Temple Beth El in Boca Raton, Florida. She complet-ed her studies at Hebrew Union College–Jewish Institute of Religion in Los Angeles in 2022, after earning her M.A. in Hebrew Letters from HUC-JIR in 2019 and a second Master's in Jewish Education in 2020. Born and raised in Los Angeles, Rabbi Rabishaw spent every summer at URJ camp OSRUI in Oconomowoc, Wisconsin. She loved summers in Wisconsin so much that she attended the University of Wisconsin-Madison, where she earned her B.Sc. in Community and Nonprofit Leadership and Modern Hebrew.

never know what story, question, or opinion you're gonna get.

On the first day of class in 2023, I felt like I had eaten the worst piece of chocolate imaginable. A twenty-something student with bright eyes and a soul full of curiosity raised her hand to get my attention. "We live in Boca Raton, Florida; there are Jews everywhere, it seems." And then, the kicker: "I am on a college campus and get this question a lot. Do we really *need* Israel?"

My heart dropped, and my emotions took over. For my entire life, there has been a strong, democratic, and vibrant State of Israel. I cannot imagine life or a world without it. Since high school, I have always thought about making Aliyah. For me, Israel's existence as a Jewish state has innately meant that I have a safe place to create a home if I ever needed or wanted. By questioning the need for Israel, I was suddenly forced to imagine how different Jewish life would be without it.

Had we really regressed to the nineteenth century?

In the nineteenth century, "the Jewish question" was a global conversation that discussed the treatment of Jews. In *The Jewish State*, Theodor Herzl considered the Jewish question "neither a social nor a religious one, even though it sometimes takes these and other forms." Essentially, the world agreed that Jews were "the Other," and Herzl's answer was that the Jewish people needed a place of their own. If the Jews could have their own state, he argued, the perspective could shift. The questions would then be about all of the possibilities in a place without antisemitism and where Jews were the majority population.

I took a deep breath, remembering I have the great blessing of living only in a time when the State of Israel existed.

I heard the song "Jerusalem of Gold" in my head. I remembered that in early 1967, while the Old City of Jerusalem was still under Jordanian occupation, the legendary songwriter Naomi Shemer used biblical imagery to write a contemporary song about her longing for Jerusalem. I felt the holiness that the paratroopers must have felt when, in June of that year, they conquered Jerusalem during the Six-Day War, and it was her words that they sang.

I saw the sunset over the Old City of Acre where, if I looked to my left, I would see families finishing their celebration of Eid. When I looked to the right, I saw the Mediterranean, and when I looked next to me, I saw my parents, with whom I was about to eat at a modern seafood restaurant owned by one of the top chefs in Israel. Acre feels like a melting pot of different religions, cultures, and walks of life. Many of the streets are so old and narrow that they are pedestrian-only. If those walls could talk, they would speak—in Hebrew, Arabic, English, Russian, German, and more—of thousands of years of stories, different from any other place in Israel.

I realized that to be a successful teacher of Judaism and Torah, I would need to begin with one of the most important lessons I learned from the great Reform-Zionist rabbi of the mid-twentieth century, Abba Hillel

Silver. He wrote in 1935 that "nation, race, land, language were always vital and indispensable concepts in Jewish life, indissolubly associated with religion. It was never a case of one or the other. They were all one, organically united." The greatness of Judaism is the seamless interweaving of these pieces. The land, state, and people of Israel are all three parts of our history, culture, and who we are.

* * *

So yes, we *need* Israel. But how do I teach love?

How do I teach feelings of love and yearning? Especially to those who do not have a connection to their Jewish roots or imagine Judaism in their home as a given.

What would happen to American Jewry if there were no dream of attending Birthright? For decades, Birthright has done an incredible job of enticing emerging Jewish adults from all backgrounds with a free trip to Israel, in which they could immerse themselves in the country and in their Judaism. While falling in love with falafel and Israeli soldiers, hundreds of thousands of Jews from diasporic communities also went on to fall in love with Judaism later in life. They were excited to return to their college campuses or synagogues with new, worldly views. And when they wanted more, these young adults innovated, developing organizations dedicated to building community for their age and stage in life, knowing that Jewish preschool would be waiting for them when they one day became parents.

When my parents met, my dad had just returned from living in Israel, and my mom was on the way to making Aliyah. Loving Israel and its people is in my blood, because it is in their blood. They taught me that I could always develop an independent Jewish identity, and that reaching Jerusalem is always a homecoming and a moment for celebration.

As one drives from Tel Aviv to Jerusalem, the last stretch of Highway 1 takes you up into the mountains, where you encounter a sign that says *bruchim habaim*, or "Welcome." There is something magical about reaching the peak of that hill. One of the first things you see in Jerusalem is the new light rail as it passes over the modern Bridge of Strings, an architectural marvel designed by the famous Spanish architect Santiago Calatrava, symbolizing Israel's technological innovation. However, surrounding the light rail are cobblestone streets that are thousands of years old. Jerusalem is the heart of where our people lived, thrived, and have ultimately grown. From this epicenter comes American Jewry, and the ability to send children to that Jewish preschool, because this home base exists.

In the nineteenth century, Naftali Herz Imber wrote the words of "Hatikvah," not to be the future national anthem of Israel but as an articulation of our collective hope of the past two thousand years for there to be a place where we—as Jews—can be "a free people in our own land." The modern State of Israel represents the actualization of this dream.

On October 7, 2023, terrorists got painfully close to taking this dream away from us. The words of "Hatikvah" must serve as a call that we can never take Israel for granted.

Ahavat yisrael, which translates to our "love of Israel," spans the historic Land of Israel to the modern State and through the entire People of Israel. For many, especially an entire generation that only knows Israel with one prime minister, this is a challenge. But true *ahavat yisrael* recognizes that the government and the country of Israel are two different things, and that peacefully protesting for your values can be both Jewish and Israeli.

* * *

Perhaps one cannot teach someone to love. What I can do, however, is share my experiences.

Like at a restaurant when one leg of a table is shaky and you place a sugar packet or a folded piece of paper under the base to stabilize it—we too require extra stabilization for our beautiful table. Now is the time for more education, to teach with love and curiosity. To someone choosing Judaism or looking to affirm their Judaism, I'd begin my answer with two words from the book of Exodus: *naaseh v'nishma*—"We will do, and then we will understand." There is nothing more Jewish than acting on faith, in the belief that understanding will ultimately follow. Just over eighteen weeks after this question was asked, the festival of Passover was upon us. The class ended, and two students joined the congregation for Seder. As the Seder ends, they say the words "Next Year in Jerusalem!" with hope, happiness, and the deep understanding that Zionism and Judaism are one.

24

Include Our Critics or We'll Lose Our Soul

Shanie Reichman

A rmchair Zionists living privileged lives in the U.S. have no right to criticize the Israeli government or military while Israelis live in a war zone"—this is a common myth that permeates the American Jewish community. It is reinforced by many Israelis, who view any criticism of Israel abroad as a betrayal of the Zionist cause.

As the director of a young-professional program that embraces individuals with a broad range of pro-Israel views, including those frequently critical of Israeli policies, I often encounter this hurtful rhetoric—and its implicit claim that we, Diaspora Jews, are not sufficiently connected to the Jewish homeland to voice our concerns about Israeli actions.

Shanie Reichman is the director of strategic initiatives and director of IPF Atid at Israel Policy Forum, based in New York City, where she works to elevate the discourse around the Israeli-Palestinian conflict, and is a frequent host of the Israel Policy Pod. Shanie serves as the founding co-chair for the Forum Dvorah U.S. committee, as a Wexner Field Fellow, a Schusterman ROIer, on the board of Queens College Hillel, on the advisory council for the Center for Ethnic, Racial and Religious Understanding, and as a mentor with Girl Security. Her work has been published in the *Forward*, the *Jerusalem Post*, *Times of Israel*, *Hey Alma*, *Jewish Unpacked*, eJewishPhilanthropy, and *International Policy Digest*.

Such a position not only silences those who are looking to engage with Israel, but also assumes that the destiny of the Jewish state somehow has no impact on that of the Jewish people, wherever they may live. Some Jewish communal leaders not only repeat this rhetoric, but have internalized it in their approach to Israel education, activism, and advocacy.

This comes at a heavy cost. Without setting up a broader tent for our Zionist Jewish community, we risk excluding the many young Jews who feel attached to Israel, but are alienated by some of its illiberal policies. The familiar trope of liberal American Jews "distancing themselves from Israel" is fast becoming a self-fulfilling prophecy. Avoiding that will require a profound change in approach from pro-Israel organizations looking to maintain the ever-critical Israel-Diaspora relationship.

* * *

In IPF Atid, the young-professional network of Israel Policy Forum, we often confront these issues head on: We encourage young adults to dig into the thorniest of issues, challenge themselves and each other, hear divergent perspectives, and use their knowledge to gain confidence in engaging with peers and colleagues who may disagree. Through these discussions emerges a theme of grappling with the starkest generational, religious, and political divides on Israel within the Jewish community, as so many struggle to navigate family WhatsApp chats, Shabbat dinners, and social media posts.

While the political leanings of the American Jewish community are stable across age groups, the older generations' long memory of an Israel that was both the underdog and represented by left-wing leaders, many of whom actively pursued peace, makes them resilient in the face of a changing Israel. Their connection will never be at risk so long as they can view Israel within the arc of history instead of focusing on the past decade.

I, however, was born two months before the November 1995 assassination of Prime Minister Yitzhak Rabin. I have little memory of an Israeli prime minister who wasn't from the center-right, and since I've followed current events it has almost always been Benjamin Netanyahu. The Israel of the Kibbutzim, of Golda Meir and Rabin, is long gone.

And while mourning those losses can be important, it's more productive to grapple with the current reality in a way that preserves the crucial relationship between American Jews and Israel. My generation and those younger than me struggle to associate Israel with many of the values that permeate American Jewry's dominant culture and institutions. Many of us find ourselves expressing concerns with Israeli policy, only to be confronted with reminders of wars fought long before we were born. Understanding and internalizing the history of the Land and State of Israel should not come at the expense of developing a mature and critical voice, when it comes to its present and future.

Attempting to differentiate the State and people of Israel from their democratically elected leaders is challenging, but can be overcome with the right framing. Fortunately, there are ample opportunities for our vibrant community to accommodate multiple views and to reignite a passion for engaging with Israel, beyond those in the traditional hasbara space.

* * *

It may seem obvious to some of us that since Israel is the homeland of the Jewish people, each and every one of us has both a right and even an obligation to be invested in its future. Over the last two and a half decades, the Jewish community has invested billions of dollars in strengthening the connection between young American Jews and the State and people of Israel. This cause is both noble and deeply vital, forming a cornerstone of our collective future. We can embrace the ideal that whatever its politics, the Diaspora can and should maintain a connection to Israel and identify with Zionism.

However, this critical relationship is now under threat, challenged by an Israeli government comprising far-right, ultra-Orthodox, and anti-pluralistic politicians. As we grapple with the disconnect between Israel's government and the 70 percent of American Jews who are liberal, there is a reluctance to rethink our approach and innovate in the way we build pro-Israel communities.

This leaves little room for common ground with liberal young American Jews, many of whom shy away from even talking about Israel today. Over the course of the Israel-Hamas war, many liberal and progressive young American Jews have felt deeply isolated as they navigate painful conversations and experience hate from the very peers, colleagues, and fellow activists they may have worked alongside for years, many of whom turned against the Jewish people as early as the day of October 7. Some of these young Jews had not been engaging with Israel at all prior to the war, but were so shocked and alienated by their progressive communities that they were compelled to seek out Jewish community in the midst of the crisis.

This tension between a right-wing Israel and a left-wing American Jewish population has been brewing for almost half a century. It has long been the case that American Jewish institutions have been unwilling to broaden the Zionist tent enough to address the diversity of Zionist thought and a broad range of perspectives. One's connection to Israel, however, need not be rooted in support of Israel's policies or military strategy, though that is how we most often see it manifest. There are countless paths to engaging deeply with Israel, including culture, language, activism, and policy (my personal favorite).

To be sure, before October 7, pro-Israel Jewish organizations had gradually begun to tolerate increasingly divergent opinions on Israel, particularly in the wake of the November 2022 election of Israel's most right-wing government in history and the anti-judicial-reform protests of the following year. That said, since the Simchat Torah Massacre, and in an effort to develop a unified voice, we've begun to fall in line. We have come to fear any dissent regarding Israel's actions, both political and military. While there is a temptation to be cautious about criticizing Israel in the middle of a war and amid the sea of antisemitic and anti-Israel discourse across the country, a nuanced approach that allows for measured and thoughtful questioning and critique would provide an outlet to those who disengage for fear of reproach, and avoid a potential backlash from those feeling silenced.

Today we are presented with a unique opportunity, as surveys show a "surge" in overall Jewish engagement in America since October 7. By embracing a broader vision of Zionism, our community can ensure inclusion and shared definitions that lead to a sense of belonging within the pro-Israel community.

A recent survey by the Jewish Federations of North America revealed a stunning fact: While 90 percent of American Jews believe Israel has a right to exist as a Jewish state, and 91 percent support Israel over Hamas in the current war, only 46 percent identify as Zionist—with another 32 percent saying they "don't know" whether they are Zionist, as well as 17 percent who call themselves "non-Zionist" (only 5 percent identify as "anti-Zionist").

It is safe to assume that those who support Israel's right to exist, but don't know whether they are Zionist, come mainly from the liberal flank of the community (though some are likely from the ultra-Orthodox community)—as do many who say they are "non-Zionist." This provides an opportunity to promote a more complex interpretation of Zionism that can lead to most of the 90 percent of American Jews who embrace Israel's right to exist as a Jewish state to identify as Zionists. My preferred definition is "support for a secure, Jewish, democratic state of Israel." Surely more than 46 percent of American Jews would support this.

A wider definition of Zionism would be, in many ways, a return to what once was. The Zionism of my grandfather's generation was centered around one goal: the establishment of a flourishing Jewish state. My grandfather's Zionism expressed itself through his learning the Hebrew language, smuggling Iraqi Jewish refugees into Mandatory Palestine in the wake of the *farhud* pogrom, raising an Israeli flag atop his synagogue in Tehran, and ultimately moving to Israel to fight in the newly created IDF. Certainly his story is an extreme example, but he coexisted, mostly peacefully, with religious Zionists, cultural Zionists, labor Zionists, and others who did not subscribe to an identical worldview of what Israel should look like, at a time when the stakes were arguably higher than they are today.

My Sabba, who ended up aligning with the Revisionist Zionism movement founded by Vladimir Jabotinsky (the forerunner of today's Likud), might have choice words for other approaches to settling the Land of Israel—but to him there was no question that we were all one community. The understanding of all the Jewish people being part of the Zionist project in its many forms will support our ability to make space in the tent for those who demand openness to questions about the current reality.

* * *

There still remains the question of how to put this broader-tent strategy into practice. One path will require the inclusion of Palestinian perspectives in our community's approach to education and dialogue. This cannot be achieved through tokenizing the few Palestinians with whom we entirely agree or who identify as pro-Israel, but rather platforming voices that make us uncomfortable. Nationwide, 81 percent of American Jews feel empathy for Palestinians (a mere 1 percent lower than the rate for non-Jewish Americans), so this should not be perceived as controversial by large swaths of the community.

Another crucial component of including the liberal camp in the Zionist discourse is building connections between Israeli and American Jews who share the values of equality, democracy, and pluralism. This solidarity movement will address a growing American-Jewish perception that Israelis are exclusively represented by their hawkish and even far-right leadership. The protest movements in Israel have done a tremendous amount to fight back against this narrative and to showcase the resilience of Israeli society and the distinction between the government and its people. If young liberal American Jews can seek out, collaborate, and build relationships with Israelis who share their values, it will highlight the contrast between Israel's government and its people—a necessary task after over a decade of Israeli leaders for whom most American Jews would never vote.

Change is always risky, particularly for a minority community like ours. And yet, we have more to lose by risking the credibility of Zionism, if it cannot contain the divergent views of many pro-Israel Jews, and even alienates those who should fit neatly into the movement but have been left out. I am heartened by my work with incredible partners at American Jewish organizations around the country who are similarly concerned with recent trends and committed to advancing a nuanced approach to Zionism and Israel programming. This leaves me hopeful that there is a growing commitment to elevating the discourse and broadening the scope of our work when it comes to Israel.

The Jewish community is generally exceptional at embracing diversity of thought on religion, philosophy, and a range of other topics. We continue the legacy of Israel's founding leaders who embodied vision and courage. Should we choose to carry the torch of those who risked their lives in the name of Jewish peoplehood and sovereignty, we will surely see a more resilient and durable Zionism, one that fulfills our obligations to the next generation of Jews around the world.

25

Zion, Our Spiritual Lifeline

Noah Shufutinsky

I'll be honest. The question of why I am a Zionist is something I never asked myself, neither before nor after I heard it used as a slur. Not before I knew how many times the word "Zion" appeared in our holy texts. Not after I set foot on the slippery Jerusalem stones that harnessed the cold winter air of January 2018.

That was the first time I'd visited Israel. Growing up, I understood the importance of the land, and I felt the connection to it from thousands of miles away. But it wasn't until a month and a half after turning eighteen that I had the chance to visit for the first time.

In the back of my mind, I had a lot of questions about what it would be like. Would it live up to my spiritual ex-

---

Noah Shufutinsky is a Jewish educator, lecturer, and musician based in Bat Yam, Israel. He earned his B.A. in Judaic Studies at the George Washington University, where he was heavily involved in Jewish life and Zionist activism. Noah is also known by his stage name, Westside Gravy. As an artist he fuses his passion for Jewish culture and history with his lived experience of growing up Black and Jewish across the United States, to write and produce hip hop. As an educator with StandWithUs, he speaks about topics regarding Israeli and Jewish history, connection to the homeland, and how antisemitism affects Jewish people around the world.

pectations, or fulfill my longing to feel at home the way it had for my older brother on his first trip? One thing I knew for sure was that generations before me had struggled to maintain and to pave the way for my own Jewish identity, and I was on my way to the center of the Jewish past.

What I didn't realize was that I was also on my way to the center of the Jewish future, collectively and personally. I was on the way to my future home, which is a weird thing to comprehend.

* * *

I grew up as a Navy brat, moving around every three years. Home for me always meant wherever I was temporarily living, as long as my family was there. But in the back of my mind I also understood that Israel was home, because it was the home of my ancestors and the shared home of my brothers and sisters. It was a strange feeling to be heading home for the first time at eighteen, not just viewing the land in a spiritual way, but as a physical place where my feet would step, my voice would echo, my nose would smell, and my eyes would see.

As a people, historically, that is where we come from. It's the genesis of the blood that courses through most of our veins and the determination that beats in all of our hearts. It's the birthplace of the synonymous syllables that exit our mouths in a variety of accents. It's the place that, regardless of how long we'd been dispersed or what conditions we'd experienced, we vowed to return to. The basis of

Zionism is that integral part of our identity that has been present in every single generation in every single Diaspora community. The longing, and action, to make a return home feasible.

Religiously, we hold the land tight in every aspect of our lives. Whether it is the direction we pray, the place where our dietary laws originate, or the plants we wave around a few days a year—just like the roots of those plants, our practices are indigenous to that ground.

But I didn't grow up with every aspect of that religious life. Like many other children of various backgrounds, my experience as the son of a Soviet Jewish refugee meant that even without those practices, my connection was equally deep.

We often hear stories of how Israel was a physical lifeline for Jews of Europe as well as of the Middle East and North Africa. The only safe haven for persecuted minorities. I want to tell a different story. I want to tell you how Zion was not just the physical lifeline, but also a spiritual lifeline.

Long before migration back to our homeland was possible, the parents and grandparents of those Mizrahi, Sephardi, and Ashkenazi refugees of the twentieth century relied on their return, their Zionism, to survive in community with one another. Zion, no matter the distance it was, helped ingather the exiles while they were still in exile.

But this isn't just a pre-twentieth century story. For my dad and families like his, who were born in a country where the regime had outlawed all Jewish practices on a basis of anti-nationalism, they in turn recognized Jewish national identity. In a world without Hebrew, Jewish holidays, kosher restaurants, thriving synagogues, and all the other benefits of Jewish life I enjoyed as a child in the United States, the thing that kept them connected to their roots was the mere knowledge that they were from Israel and would someday return.

That was in 1981. Fast forward thirty-seven years, and I was in the midst of that return. So the question of why I am a Zionist isn't something I could ever fathom asking; it's something ingrained in the story of every Jew born into our tribes and every Jew who spiritually returns to our ranks by adopting the practices of our nation. It's the homecoming I had at eighteen, that I unknowingly longed for.

* * *

While I have never looked for a cut-and-dry answer to that question, I have been forced to find an answer for people unfamiliar with that story. The story they are familiar with isn't one of an indigenous people returning to their brothers and sisters in the land they were born of. It's a false narrative of white-European-settler-colonialism that my very existence interferes with. Nevertheless, this narrative has penetrated all aspects of society, from college professors in lecture halls like the ones I sat in not too long ago to entertainment awards shows, from newsrooms to Instagram stories of everyone's favorite musician—or a washed-up one with a decades-old hit about finding cheap clothing.

This challenge has required me not just to find my answer as to why I am a Zionist, but to find the specific quality necessary to convey my answer. What is required is a healthy dose of *unapologeticism*, which is sometimes viewed as unhealthy in today's world. But unapologeticism begets respect. In a world where everything has to have a grey area, we often try to find it even in the black-and-white. It's a good thing to look for dialogue and nuance, but certain things are not up for debate.

So when I take a trip down memory lane, which isn't that long of a road for someone of my age, I think back to my first few days on campus. My peers who heard that I'm Jewish immediately questioned me regarding my opinions on Zionism and Israel. And I went out of my comfort zone and what I knew in my heart, to present a very neutral perspective on the area—explaining that I loved my homeland but also had disagreements with its policies.

For far too long, that is the answer Jews in my generation have been trained to give: one of reaction rather than action, an answer of being poised to apologize for an accusation not yet leveled. We want friends, we want to sound reasonable, and we look for concessions we can make to those who despise us.

My answer today, however, is much simpler. It is thoroughly unapologetic. It was upon walking the streets in Israel that I realized the results of these concessions and the grave danger of compromising on the central fact that Israel is our home. The stories I'd learned about refugees having nowhere to go except home became real and human. The soldiers who had lost friends for the sake of our homeland did not put their lives on the line out of concessions. They did so out of pure love and commitment to our nation that originates in this land, as well as the idea that affirms our right to live as a free people here.

This commitment sometimes gives way to compromise. I met Israelis who believed in a two-state solution, one-state solution, and everything in between. Some agreed with my positions, some disagreed, but the basis of their opinions was not based in concessions. This same approach has to be adopted in the Diaspora on the ideological battlefield.

That shaped my answer into what it is today. Israel is my home. It's where my people are from and where we have succeeded in returning to. It's where I am rarely questioned regarding my appearance as a Black Jew, and where my identity is not tokenized for a political point. It's the land that gives me the inspiration I need to make freedom songs—not those longing for liberation or lamenting a loss of it, but songs representing what a free Jew looks and sounds like. Whether it's a love song in Hebrew, a political manifesto in musical form, or even just instrumentation playing melodies that have developed in this land over thousands of years, and today remind listeners of the origins of our prayers—this is the sound of freedom. The sound of a Jew unchained and able to express himself fully, rather than having his identity confined to a reaction to a false narrative. A Jew whose voice resonates within the walls of his home and flows out of open windows beyond the surrounding city, into the countryside.

Our Zionism isn't a reaction to bigotry or policies. It's the story of who we are, beginning with where we are from, documenting how we got to everywhere we've been, and ending with where we will always be. Home.

26

How I Went from Pro-Israel Activist to "Zionist Being"

Sabrina Soffer

I vividly remember my father's perplexing words: how he wanted to "kiss the ground" each time we disembarked at Ben-Gurion airport, stepping onto the sacred soil of the Jewish homeland. Like the wicked son at the Passover Seder, I would ask, "What is the meaning of all this to *you*?" Summer after summer, I would say, "Why Israel? We have to go *again*?"

Invariably my father would respond: "Just you wait, you'll understand me when you're older. It'll hit you one day."

And as usual, my father was right. In my second year of college, I became a Zionist.

At first, the anti-Zionism I experienced in college was every bit as perplexing as my father's infatuation with

Sabrina Soffer is the former commissioner of the Task Force to Combat Antisemitism at George Washington University, where she is majoring in Philosophy and Public Affairs and Judaic Studies. She is the vice president of Chabad GW and served as the Chair of Hillel International's Content Creators Program in 2023-2024. Her writings have appeared *The Hill* and *The Jerusalem Post*. She is the author of *My Mother's Mirror: A Generational Journey of Resilience & Self-Discovery* (2022).

Israel. I didn't understand the meaning behind slurs like "colonial apologist," "racist oppressor," and "right-wing extremist" when I proudly shared my Israeli background and Jewish roots with fellow students in my freshman year. Determined to understand these accusations and to defend myself, I pursued an academic exploration of such phrases, their history and evolution.

It became clear that anti-Zionism and antisemitism historically, whether in the Middle East or in Europe, were the products of religious authorities and authoritarian leaders indoctrinating their populace with what to think rather than how to think, steering them toward a political goal. College, I quickly understood, was no different: The intellectual culture was dominated by an authoritarian, oppressor-oppressed binary worldview, where anti-Israel sentiment was a given and *always* resulted in hostility toward Jews.

Confronting the irrationality and persistence of antisemitic ideologies that have plagued Jewish communities for centuries evoked a profound sense of purpose within me, spurring me to challenge adversaries of the Jewish people. In doing so, I found my Jewish identity and love for Israel fortified in ways I had never experienced before.

But while anti-Zionism and antisemitism may have lit my Zionist fire, they fell short of infusing Zionism into my being. After several months of battling campus antisemitism did I start to think more deeply about my relationship with Zionism itself. What did Zionism mean to me? Why was I asking this only now?

* * *

Indeed, I had allowed the anti-Zionists to create the notion of the Zionist that I was. Realizing that approaching problems reactively rather than proactively was saturating me with negativity and unproductive results, I had to shift my approach from merely being a strong Zionist to embodying a *Zionist Being*.

The most important element of a Zionist Being is gratitude. In my frequent daydreams about Israel, I often consider what would become of me without the Jewish homeland. The answer is that I likely would not be here, on this earth, at all. Israel was my family's ticket to protection and prosperity, and thus my own. Many Jews around the world today can tell similar stories.

My appreciation for Israel and admiration for Zionism, however, transcend the physical boundaries of land, family, and the Israeli people. Israel is the birthplace of my values and ethics: work ethic, will, debate, compromise, confidence, and collective good. Israel is consistently reborn and reinvented through diverse *aliyot* that have shaped its society and contributions to the world.

Israel reflects what every human being should aspire toward, embodying a beacon of success. Not just economic, technological, or military success, but true success—authentic happiness: Aristotelian happiness, or *eudaimonia*, achieved by attaining fulfillment through striving toward a higher purpose, even if the path there is not easy. In a country where family is the civic religion and life is the utmost value, the paramount purpose lies in pursuing a meaningful existence marked by continuous progress.

While Jewish tradition imparts principles for leading a life of significance, in Israel, the pursuit of meaning is of utmost value because of its small community and intimate, most tragic familiarity with mortality. In Israel, *kulam mishpacha*—everyone is family. With the survival of the Jewish future intricately tied to the resilience of Israel, Israelis possess a remarkable ability to transform obstacles into opportunities while upholding their spirit in the darkest of times. For the Zionist future to live the post-October-7 mantra "we will dance again," we must internalize Israel's wisdom that morale in battle is just as, if not more, important than the battle itself.

*** *** ***

In Israel, literal battles are commonplace and can be existential. Outside Israel, other battles, like the global mental health crisis, overwhelm our society. While different in nature, the same principles embodied in a Zionist Being apply to fighting them.

Throughout my life, I have dealt with debilitating stress and anxiety that transformed into physical ailments such as hair-pulling (a condition known as trichotillomania) and crippling stomach pains. Mental health issues, no matter their specific cause, often stem from misperceptions and being mired in insignificant things. Amid my cycles of anxiety, I tended to fixate on trivial matters like completing a homework assignment, an exam grade, or my dream college, while my mood soured toward my friends and family. I lost sight of what really mattered, drowning deep in a crisis of meaning.

Looking to Israel as a model of resilience has enabled me to resolve the crisis of meaning that once plagued me. In college, I have grown indifferent to superficial accolades and sources of instant gratification. Digging into my family history and heritage has enabled me to cultivate invaluable connections with my grandparents from Egypt and Dagestan who immigrated to Israel for protection and prosperity. This exploration has brought me closer to my family's Kafkazi, Arab, and Israeli Jewish roots—and thus to myself, through an appreciation for my personal history and the country that helped my family survive and thrive. Such an appreciation has allowed me to learn for learning's sake with an eye on the continuity of my heritage and people. Knowing what we're living for invests meaning in the present. As one of my friends has remarked, learning about Zionism "was better than therapy."

Hard work toward a higher purpose leads to the best results. During this process, individuals may also learn to value the struggle itself, freeing their minds of dread and negativity in the face of challenges. Setting on a higher purpose with profound awareness of values, beliefs, and actions also builds a defense against those who try to deter us. Israel is a reflection of such principles, and has taught us that peace—of mind or of physical security—can be achieved only through strength.

Resolute in Jewish identity and commitment to purpose, Zionism remains open to compromise and collaboration under certain conditions. Just as the biblical Noah, Abraham, Moses, and David forged a principled covenant with God, I've developed a covenant-like relationship with Zionism through my Israel advocacy. This relationship is symbiotic. Just as our forebears' covenant with God endowed them with values to lead their lives and their people, my commitment to Zionism has created the opportunities to cultivate my character and conduct.

I tend to imagine the Zionist pioneers as a single human vessel that has spanned the time and space of Jewish history. As this individual yearned and returned to her ancient homeland while experiencing harsh enmity, she has been able to develop an incessant drive toward her dreams. Like a true hero, Zionism never backs down. I have been called the "most hated Jew on campus," and I have discovered that being hated can actually be liberating. Freedom arrives with confidence in my beliefs, values, and actions no matter the reactions of the outside. With each hateful allegation, I can only ask myself what is wrong with what I stand behind. The answer is nothing, and with that answer, I reaffirm confidence in my Zionism and Israeli-Jewish identity, realizing that the character traits packaged with who I am are worthy of being amplified.

Not unlike my childhood, when I was perplexed at my father's Zionism, a great many Jews living in the Diaspora have grown comfortable and assimilated, ignoring their roots and growing indifferent to both Judaism and

Zionism. Antisemitism, faults in Jewish education, or the apathy toward religion in modern society may all help explain it—but the indifference that results is what matters. To paraphrase Holocaust survivor and Nobel Laureate Elie Wiesel, indifference can prove more threatening than hatred because, as in the context of the Holocaust, forgetting would be akin to killing the Jews a second time.

In the aftermath of October 7, when unthinkable tragedy befell the Jewish people yet again, we have witnessed a resurgence of Jewish identity, pride, and exploration. Jewish pride, however, cannot continue to depend on waves of persecution. Instead, it must come from within, from an intrinsic desire to build a relationship with our national, ethnic, and religious identities. Such a process may be unique on an individual level, but the universal principles derived from Zionism, and especially its core of *principled personal responsibility*, can ignite this spark and help us extend it to all aspects of life.

These three words—*principled, personal,* and *responsibility*—should be infused into young Jews today.

Like our Zionist forebears committed to determining a solution for a Jewish national destiny, young Zionists must carry the *principle* of purpose to survive and thrive to sustain it: both as a people and as individuals. Furthermore, this principle demands the Herzlian notion of unity, not uniformity, in robust discussion, debate, and development, to ensure that the best ideas for the Jewish future rise to the top.

The *personal* element is embedded in knowing our story—our own, our family, and that of our people—to gain insight into who we are as individuals and a collective. For ourselves, knowing our story evokes a strong sense of Jewish identity never to be disavowed, and sharing our story with others can forge relationships that transcend national, ethnic, and religious divides.

Lastly, we bear the *responsibility* of integrating our principles and personal narratives into our daily lives, thereby nurturing strong character. Drawing from Zionist ideals centered on purpose, progress, and projection, we cultivate personal confidence while fostering meaningful connections with others by normalizing Judaism and Zionism.

To truly serve as a light unto nations, we cannot allow our Jewish pride or strategic endeavors to be solely reactive. As Jonathan Kessler, the founder and CEO of Heart of a Nation, expressed to me, we cannot merely act as firefighters, tirelessly extinguishing every flame ignited by Israel's adversaries and antisemites. Instead, we must "fight the fire by fortifying the forest," rendering ourselves impermeable to these external assaults.

In line with the wisdom of Sun Tzu, "Know thyself and thy enemy, a thousand battles, a thousand victories," we recognize that intimate self-knowledge is the key to triumph in our endeavors. Understanding ourselves entails embodying the timeless principles embedded in our heritage and derived from our collective history—principles that we are duty-bound to execute. We must create a Zionist future defining ourselves by the principles that have shaped and strengthened us, fighting for and through them.

27

Home, Transcendence, and the Land

Julia Steinberg

While discussing my upcoming trip to Israel, my good, *goyish* friend started her sentence with, "If you come back...." This was December 2022—a year before the war, a year before "Zionist" became a slur, a year before I started hanging an Israeli flag from my dorm room window.

She had just finished reading *The Counterlife* by Philip Roth for a class on Zionism that I had also taken the previous spring. The novel guides the reader through different realities and histories crafted by Jewish author Nathan Zuckerman, a fictionalized version of Roth himself. For that class, I wrote my final paper on a character in the book named Jimmy Lustig, a Zuckerman superfan from New Jersey. Jimmy, "high as a kite on Jewish commitment" and a student at the Diaspora Yeshiva in Jerusalem, first meets Zuckerman near the Western Wall. About fifty pages later, Lustig attempts a plane hijacking to raise awareness of his

Julia Steinberg is a senior at Stanford University studying comparative literature, where most of her coursework has focused on intellectual history. She is the Editor-in-Chief of the *Stanford Review* and an intern at *The Free Press*. She has also testified in front of the U.S. Senate on the issue of antisemitism on college campuses.

mission: forgetting the Holocaust.

Jimmy Lustig's manifesto calls for a new Zionism, one without Western Walls and Holocaust Museums: "FOR-GET REMEMBERING! I demand of the Israel government the immediate closing and dismantling of Yad Vashem, Jerusalem's Museum and Remembrance Hall of the Holocaust. I demand this in the name of the Jewish future. THE JEWISH FUTURE IS NOW."

Abandoning a Jewish history of victimhood in favor of an exclusive focus on Jewish future is, of course, the cry of a diasporic view. Lustig's manifesto is little more than effectively ripping up the flag of Israel, its design resembling the traditional *tallit*, entangled with the three-thousand-year history of the Jewish people and the search for salvation in the homeland. Jimmy's new Zionism calls for the destruction of all that is sacred, all the markers that create a nation—a destruction of memory.

Most scholars of nationalism agree that a shared memory is what creates a nation. Anthony Smith, a pioneer of nationalism studies, summarizes that "nationalisms are so often accompanied and fueled by the labors of intellectuals intent on tracing the 'roots' and 'character' of the nation through such disciplines as history, archaeology, anthropology, sociology, linguistics, and folklore." Whether this memory is rooted in the land, as argued by the school known as the primordialists, or manufactured in modernity, as per the modernist school, is a second question. Primordialists present as proof the existence of longstanding nationalist myths; modernists point out that they *are* myths. Either way, the history is worth remembering.

Of course, I had no idea how to parse out the history of Israel, having never set foot there. It is easy to fall in love with an idea in the Diaspora. At that point, I had read Benedict Anderson's *Imagined Communities* and understood nationalist projects as the construction of new worlds. People create "nations," he argued, through kinship bonds with other people in their community by crafting an imagined sense of general identity: "Yes, it is quite accidental that I am born French; but after all, France is eternal." But Anderson—prophet of the modernist school of nationalism—fell short in explaining Israel. Israel is very much *not* eternal— from its independence in 1948, it has always faced existential threats. And that's not even to mention the constant threats to Jewry until then. Israelis—Jews—know that their fate is precarious and worth fighting for. It is not accidental that I was born Jewish; my ancestors fought tooth and nail for the chance of my existence.

Regardless, I had bought into the modernist fad. I, born in the Jewish Cedars-Sinai Hospital in Beverly Hills like all the other assimilated Jews I knew back home, was excited to place myself in this imagined world. Roth—Zuckerman—realizes that though "I hadn't seen anything really of what Israel was…I had at least begun to get an idea of what it could be made *into* in the minds of a small number of its residents" (italics in original). I couldn't imagine the Zionist project, a more tangled ball of Play-Doh, any other way.

* * *

After I bid my friend goodbye and boarded my flight to Tel Aviv, I arrived in Israel to study military history, on a trip led by Berkeley political science professor Ron Hassner. Tel Aviv is, in some ways, the anti-Jerusalem. Constructed on a manmade tell in 1909, the city is hypermodern. I drank iced lattes strolling through indie bookstores and beachfront bars, enjoying the feeling of walking around and being surrounded by Jews. Coming from Los Angeles, where Jews hide their Jewishness via nose jobs and blonde hair dye, and then Stanford, where being Jewish *was*, before the war, uninteresting, it was a novel feeling to be surrounded by Jews. Tel Aviv was a break from history, a place where Jews, unfettered by history, could go on as normal.

This break from history to create a city of the future—one with the background noise of a resuscitated language—is not unique. Most major cities are alike in their destruction of the past to pave the way for the future. Friedrich Nietzsche, in his essay "On the Utility and Liability of History for Life," declared that overly concerning oneself with history was a vehicle for "withdrawal from life and action" and is only "the grave digger of the present." A successful modern state, then, must face forward. Forget monuments and museums and national holidays.

One of my first stops in Israel was at Gymnasia Herzliya Hebrew High School, the country's first Hebrew high school. It is in a new building (the original, founded in

1905, was razed to build the then-tallest building in Israel, in true futurist fashion) and taught in newly-resuscitated Hebrew. The project of the school was to unite the future Jewry in our ancestral language, to reunite the Jewish Diaspora in building a new nation.

Though my Hebrew is shoddy at best, while walking around Tel Aviv, dancing with a Russian Jew on New Year's Eve to house music, eating at trendy Italian restaurants, smoking cigarettes with leftist students at Tel Aviv University, I was a *modern* Jew.

We spent only the first day of the trip galivanting around Tel Aviv. The aim, again, was to study military history, in many ways the opposite of the cultural history that Nietzsche lampoons. Jimmy's attempted plane hijacking was a failed attempt at the violence that marked the battlefields we saw—in crusader castles, Megiddo, the Golan, Acre, the Valley of Tears. And, for the last leg of the trip, we toured the battlefields of Jerusalem, perhaps the most fought-over city in the world.

Our first full day in Jerusalem started by crawling through millennia-old Canaanite tunnels, likely used to protect the ancient city. Our next stop was the Western Wall—to me, until then, a postcard picture.

I can't say I did anything but break down once I reached the Kotel—the Western Wall, the holiest site of Judaism. My grandparents, who met in Israel, left for America before the 1967 Six-Day War when Israel, victorious, took control over the Western Wall, the last remnants of the lost Temple. Neither of my parents had ever been there. I cried with the weight on my shoulders that I was likely the first in my bloodline for thousands of years to see the holiest site in Judaism. I suddenly felt that *not going back* to California, the edge of the world, from the center, Jerusalem, was a very real option. Something told me to stay. I had never felt that way before in *any* location, let alone halfway across the world.

The Western Wall is the heart of Jerusalem's Old City. Our textbook for the study abroad course, Karen Armstrong's *Jerusalem: One City, Three Faiths*, maps how the city has expanded through conquest, destruction, and rebuilding. Late in the book's chronology, Armstrong describes how Jews "seem to have turned to the vacant stretch of the western wall of the Haram, clinging to it as their last link with the past." It was indeed the last link to our ancient civilization, whose nucleus—King David's capital—was not far from this wall in Jerusalem. As Jerusalem came back under Jewish control in 1967, the last remains of ancient Jewish civilization were refurbished as the spiritual epicenter of the modern Jewish nation.

Surrounded by Orthodox women and other bawling Americans, I felt home in a way I never had. I had a mild case, perhaps, of Jerusalem syndrome, without the religious hallucinations or the need to be checked into a hospital. Prompted by seeing—feeling—the Western Wall, I felt a sense of place and permanence and strength that I had never felt before.

* * *

I knew that something in me changed when I saw the Kotel, but I couldn't put my finger on it. I felt shaken. And though I had some connection to Israel, I felt like a case study when I reflected on my time at the Western Wall. The shared memory of a people, drawn to its anchor yet held at bay, welled up in my soul.

I regained my composure, and off we went, wandering around the Old City—seeing apartments and storefronts inhabited by Jews who had, like me, *returned* to the land, their people (my people) having lived there thousands of years ago. A shopkeeper, an American who had made Aliyah, gave my friend and me *hamsa* necklaces and told us to call him if we were to return.

A few weeks later, I went to Washington, D.C., for the first time for a conference, one of many post-fleeting-Israel-trip obligations. As a proud American who had lived in the United States for all of my twenty-one years, I was expecting to feel something similar to how I felt when I saw the Western Wall.

I did not. Though I was moved by the famous neo-classical buildings, the monuments to the world-changing promise that America represented, there was a lack of deeper feeling that could not be explained away by theorists. America, as it is now, is exempt from primordial nationalism—most Americans, Natives aside, do not have an age-old connection with the land. In Israel, I felt crazy for my own discovered connection to the Land—Volkish and old-fashioned, ashamed that I was giving credence to the nationalism that, when turned extreme, was the justification of forcing out my ancestors.

* * *

The week of October 7, I barely left my room. I ordered an Israeli flag and hung it from my dorm room window. I thought seriously about dropping out and doing the ever-vague "something to help," even joining the IDF to *defend that land*. Instead I chose to stay with my studies. The next quarter, I enrolled in a class on nationalism.

I went into the class not expecting to learn so much as to diagnose what had happened to me that early January day when I broke down in front of the Western Wall. In the first weeks, we studied the primordial view of nationalism. Johann Gottfried Herder, for example, wrote that there was a strong national character:

> Every fatherland, already just with its
> sweet name, has a *moral tendency*. It de-
> scends from *fathers*; with the name father
> it brings to our minds the recollection of
> our *times of youth* and *games of youth*; it
> awakens the memory of all the men of
> merit before us, of all the worthy men af-
> ter us to whom we will become fathers.

The moral tendency is imbued within the land itself. The Jewish spirit is imbued within *that* land. Isn't that quite blood-and-soil-ish, I asked myself? I argued with myself in my notebook during class. I tried to write counter-arguments to Herder and the other primordialists, worried that I would fall into some trap. But, despite everything, I felt myself drawn to the nation as the reflection of the land itself. Writing about England, one of the final authors we read in the class, Roger Scruton, warded off these blood-and-soil tendencies.

But who are *we*? This is the question that the English never needed to ask themselves—not because they had a ready answer, but because England exerted so strong a hold over their imaginations that they instinctively knew who they were, without recourse to those concepts of nationhood, *Volk*, and culture which have played such a large and questionable part in continental politics. England defined their membership.

If you come from the land, you are of it. Though my ancestors wandered throughout Europe, they felt *home* in Israel. It was an instinctual feeling, not a debate to be had about what defined Jewishness. My feeling in Israel was a sense of completion, a sense that I knew who I was. "Home is not just a place," Scruton wrote, "it is also what goes on there. A place *becomes* a home, by virtue of the habits that domesticate it."

The Jews were not the first and certainly have not been the only group to "domesticate" what is now Israel. But I felt—I knew—that I was cut from Israel's cloth. And that transcendent knowledge cannot be argued away.

28

Zionism Is Resilience

Asher Stern

Zionism is more than just a crucial confirmation of our Jewish identity. It is a demonstration of our people's resilience, offering a beacon of hope for the future. It is also a call to action, a summons to dialogue both within our people and with others, and a rallying cry.

While that rallying cry is based on a sense of pride in who we are and our historical physical connection to Israel, the journey of Zionism transcends geography. It is a journey of the heart, of belonging, and of self-discovery. Above all, however, it is a journey that embraces the Jewish quality of resilience. Through their resilience, Jews have found the ability to overcome. Zionism is, above all, the expression of the unique Jewish resolve to overcome.

In my case, it is also the journey of an orphan from South Africa to his people, a new family in Israel, and adding a new link to a chain that goes back thousands of years.

Asher Stern is a strategic project manager in the fields of public diplomacy, public relations, international relations, Israel and the Middle East, antisemitism, Zionism, and countering the BDS movement. Asher has a B.A. from Reichman University in Government Strategy and Diplomacy and an M.A. in International Relations from Hebrew University. His writings have appeared in *The Hill, New York Daily News, City Journal, Jerusalem Post,* JNS, *Times of Israel, Israel Hayom* (English and Hebrew), and more.

* * *

My journey began with the first time I spoke in front of my synagogue in South Africa. I was twelve. Like many young Jewish boys and girls, I had anticipated standing in front of the congregation to share my Bar Mitzvah prayer and speech. But just a few months shy of my thirteenth birthday, I found myself at the pulpit to say the mourner's prayer for my mother, who had passed away unexpectedly. While my friends were all learning their Torah portions and preparing for their celebrations, I was studying the traditions of death and mourning. While they were becoming adults according to the traditional Jewish aspirations for every child, I became an adult because my childhood was taken from me.

In the wake of my mother's death, my father and I were forced to reevaluate everything. He questioned his choice of which hospital to send my mom to, and we both questioned the decision to move to Cape Town, believing more could have been done elsewhere. There was one idea, however, that while postponed for a few years, did not waver: We were going home. Not the home in Cape Town where I grew up, but the home for which we as a people had yearned for two thousand years. We were making Aliyah.

Moving to a new country is never easy, no matter how connected you feel to its history and legacy. Doing so at age fifteen, while still mourning the loss of your mother, but needing to be strong for your father who never truly recovered from her death, makes it even harder. My dad was meant to be the adult, but he was so broken by grief that he couldn't function. So, my first three years in Israel followed a difficult routine of school, studying Hebrew, trying to make friends, and also working part-time to help put food on our table.

But, as the old saying goes and as I echoed in my Bar Mitzvah speech, "Man proposes, God disposes."

One Saturday night just before I turned eighteen—the other major landmark of adulthood—I walked into the kitchen and found my father choking. I tried to do the Heimlich maneuver, called an ambulance, and did all I could think of, but to no avail. He passed three days later. Just like that, I was alone.

***

I was forced at that moment to make a choice, one that would affect the rest of my life: Do I bend, or do I break? Essentially, I was confronted with a version of the question that the Jewish people have faced innumerable times throughout history. How do you go forward when it feels like the world is telling you not to? How do you go forward alone?

I was, fortunately, not truly alone. I was blessed with friends who would become family, both figuratively and literally—a family of incredibly special individuals who took me in, and who have been my home and my family ever since. They even walked me down the aisle when I got married and started building my family anew.

But more than that, I was motivated forward for the

same reason Jews across the ages have kept going. We were Zionists, and we had a home.

Home meant the land of our forefathers, the land that so many generations had dreamed of returning to, the land of our people. In so many ways, our people and our country had provided me with a home, a family, and a purpose.

I could not break because I still had to give back to my country. I could not dream of taking the exemption the army offered me, as an orphan, because I needed to serve and was proud to do so, in air defense. My parents had dreamed that our family would build a future together in Israel. I could not abandon that dream.

I realized, standing in Israel, in the land that was the guiding light for my people for centuries, that I am not unique in refusing to let my story break or define me, nor am I unique in being rebuilt through my connection to Israel. Rather, I am just one link in the chain of the Jewish people and Zionism.

* * *

Our identity is woven through a history both painful and joyful—a history that goes back to Abraham, through slavery in Egypt and a brief return home to Israel. We built temples, watched their destruction, and saw our people exiled to the four corners of the earth, where we not only survived but thrived. While we took on aspects of the countries we lived in, our commitment to Zion never faded. We longed for Jerusalem, a longing that expressed itself through in-

numerable prayers, songs, rabbinic tales, and countless pil-
grimages to the land of our fathers.

Growing up in South Africa, despite many trials and
tribulations (including a government currently at the forefront of antisemitic rhetoric and support for Hamas, going
so far as to bring a frivolous lawsuit against Israel in the
International Court of Justice), in the wake of October 7,
there were a few core ideas that every Jewish South African
knew, no matter their level of Jewish engagement.

When we pray, we pray towards Jerusalem. Every Passover Seder ends with "Next Year in Jerusalem!" Our people's anthem, "Hatikvah" ("The Hope"), is sung in Jewish
schools after the South African anthem. It was in these and
other aspects of our lives that those of us in exile made sure
always to raise our families with the same hope and prayer
in our hearts: to return home.

Moving to Israel, our home rebuilt after thousands
of years, I was exposed for the first time to so many other
types of Jews; Israel is truly the ingathering of the exiles. I
discovered Jews from all over the world, all of whom had
their pasts and their baggage, both good and bad. Against
all odds, the unification of all these different communal stories has created something beautiful: a Jewish state.

* * *

A Jewish state in 2024 is something that should never
have been possible. A Jewish people that maintained a connection to this land and to each other for thousands of years

should never have been possible. What our people endured should have broken us and made us forget who we were. And yet, we stood strong.

This was the people I was blessed to be a part of. A people who did not break. A people who, no matter what, kept alive the belief in coming home.

Now more than ever, we as young Jews, the current torchbearers of our history, must realize that our destiny is in our hands. It was Theodor Herzl who said, "If you will it, it is no dream." It is our turn to interpret his words as the gift that they were: the power to shape the destiny, once again, of our people and nation. To build a future that is rooted in pride, connection, and responsibility.

We are at a unique point in history. In part because of the pain we share, as well as the sense of unity we are all feeling, we can, at this moment, look both to the past and the future, to see that our connection to Israel and our people is spiritual, emotional, and existential. It is beyond time and space. It links us not only to the land of our forefathers but to their history, as well as to the hopes and dreams that we now have the honor to make real.

Through Zionism, we take on a profound responsibility to engage in dialogue and to foster understanding, both among ourselves and with the rest of the world. We must ensure that our deepest divisions, like those we saw before October 7, are not allowed to tear us apart. We have a responsibility to confront the complexities that come with being such a diverse people, and to grapple with those nuances in a manner that builds rather than destroys. It is in that quest, the ultimate quest for unity, that we must not shy away from voices that don't sound like ours, from perspectives that seem like oil to our water. We must look at those on the "other side" and embrace them. We must realize that we all care about our people and our future deeply, and must come together in a spirit of collective growth, learning, and improvement.

✱ ✱ ✱

My story, so similar to that of my people, is one of survival against the odds, of perseverance through persecution, exile, and adversity, all while maintaining an unwavering bond with our ancestral homeland, a bond woven so deeply into our prayers and ancestral memories.

It is this resilience, this unwavering commitment to our heritage, that defines us as a people and creates our collective identity. For us as young Jews, this journey is more pertinent now than ever before. In embracing Zionism at a time when so many of us feel pressure to repudiate it, we declare that despite our differences, we are united and proud. It is exactly during times of uncertainty and adversity that our shared identity as Jews and Zionists may sustain us. We must look to it to give us the strength, resilience, and determination to persevere. This is the unique challenge of our generation, and it will set the course of our people's future.

29

Living and Dying with Jewish Dignity

Sahar Tartak

When an anti-Israel tent encampment sprung up at Yale, I wasn't surprised. By then, the Jewish community at Yale had seen celebrations of the October 7 atrocities from students and professors, rallies calling for a global Intifada, and Jews barred from campus events and spaces.

For me, the culmination of the encampment took place on a Saturday night, when I was encircled and followed by a screaming mob at a midnight rally—until a masked demonstrator assaulted me in the eye with a Palestinian flag. I spent the rest of the evening in the hospital, where I was heartened to see a spark of Jewish unity. Many Jewish friends, including some who had joined the protests, reached out, wishing me a speedy recovery. For a moment,

---

Sahar Tartak is an undergraduate at Yale University. Originally from Great Neck, New York, she studies History with a concentration in Law, Government, and Politics. Last summer, she collected an oral history of the Jewish community in Athens and wrote about how the community was rebuilt after the Holocaust. She has written about Jewish life on campus and stood up for the Jewish people in the *Wall Street Journal*, the *Free Press*, the *Washington Free Beacon*, Tablet, *National Review*, the *Yale Daily News*, and the *Yale Free Press*, where she served as editor in chief. She also testified to Congress about her experiences as a Jewish student in the wake of October 7.

they shared in what the next generation of young Jews so desperately needs right now: Jewish family.

When Jews are a family, we stand up for and protect each other. We refuse to stand by and watch each other get hurt, and we certainly never identify with our abusers. We respect our ancestors and love their traditions. We stand united as one—in dignity, in loyalty, and in love.

* * *

I was most immersed in the Jewish family one night during the 2024 spring break, when I spent a few minutes standing before a mass grave of Jewish children in Poland. Around them was a small fence to mark the grave's boundaries, but I doubt it was accurate. Inside the fence was a small table of memorial candles and toys, and along the fence were balloons with children's names on them.

I stood at the fence and kneeled, and I began to speak to the children. I promised them that I'd live in their *zchut*, their merit, and that I'd raise my own children in their memory.

Eighty years before, local Polish priests heard the waning screams of girls and boys buried alive for days in that forest and did nothing. I wanted to read the children Jewish stories and tell them about Jewish life, for they had known only Jewish death. I wanted the children to know that they have a living, breathing Jewish family that cares about them.

I couldn't bring myself to lift my head from the grave. But there were sixty other college students on the trip to Poland, and the leaders of our trip beckoned us back toward the bus to retire for the night. I would have stayed all night, whispering to the children.

A few hours to the east, my great-grandmother Leah, her daughter Tziporah, and her son Adam are buried in a mass grave no different from this one, except it may not be as well marked. They're in a field somewhere in western Ukraine. I wish I could go and tell them that I'm going to name my Jewish kids after them, and I'll stay with them all night to talk.

Further still to the south, my grandfather Avraham and his father Yisroel are buried in the Har Hamenuchot cemetery in Jerusalem. They escaped the fate of their loved ones in Europe. Yet when I visited my grandfather's grave this summer, I had the same wish: to stay forever and share with him the Jewish light of today, promising that I would carry it into tomorrow. The tombstones at Har Hamenuchot are large. I lay down on his tombstone and embraced it, as if I were hugging him, and whispered about his beautiful, living Jewish family, until my mother said it was time to go.

His tombstone is marked with a verse from Genesis: "And Abraham arose early in the morning to the place where he had stood before the Lord."

In the next verse, Abraham looked out toward Sodom and Gomorrah, and "the smoke of the land went up as the smoke of a furnace." Just like our forefather Abraham, so too did my grandfather Avraham look out into the world and see the furnace. Endless other Jews have all seen the furnace, but despite the flames, they have marched on with dignity.

The sixty other college students on my Poland trip, who chose to spend a precious spring break in the cold land of death, all knew that they had seen the furnace on October 7. We all reflected on what we saw in Poland throughout the week, and could not help but draw comparisons to our campuses. No one told us to think this way. We just saw it: Among our classmates were the Nazis of today. Considering their strange admiration for the furnace, what else could we call them? They want to see our family in flames—the same flames that produced Jewish ashes in Poland, ashes used to fertilize the fields.

***

Organized by Chabad on Campus, the Poland trip was attended by students from a range of Jewish backgrounds: Some had no knowledge of Hebrew, others prayed three times a day. What we had in common was an admiration and respect for traditional Jewish life, which we understood to be the highest aspiration of Jewish existence. Sure, the students formed cliques, but no clique could resist approaching the warm *madrichot* (counselors) or our trip rabbi. It didn't matter that they looked or lived differently. We were led by loving Jews who loved us *as* Jews, which was something we could not find on campus.

During Shabbat, we students all committed to taking on new *mitzvot*, or Jewish commandments, when we returned from the trip. Our shared intuition was simple: The Jewish tradition provides a path that honors our ancestors—a path of wisdom, dignity, and faith that they died for. Emaciated Jews in the camps had given up precious hours of sleep to wake up before roll call and wrap smuggled tefillin. So for us, taking on a *mitzva* was a privilege.

At Majdanek, a concentration camp where the highest number of Jews were killed in any single day during the war, our rabbi recounted an episode that illustrated how Jews in the camp celebrated Passover. A Jewish child who had miraculously survived the selection upon arrival sang the traditional four questions. After the first question was sung, a Nazi guard threw open the barrack doors and pointed the barrel of his gun inside, threatening to mow down the room with his rifle if they continued. When he closed the door, the prisoners, including the child, kept singing. Whether atheist or devout, all agreed to continue the Seder.

This year, that same Jewish child, a Chabadnik named Nissen Mangel, took a picture outside of the Auschwitz tracks. He stood, together with his family, including more than a hundred living descendants.

＊＊＊

Unlike at Auschwitz, on campus my Jewish peers struggle to find the clarity that the students on this trip shared. Even my pro-Israel friends cannot connect the dots between our enemies of today and our enemies of the past. They privately excuse chants of "Intifada" and "river to the sea" as words that our peers just don't understand: *They don't know what those slogans mean.* Other times, they seek "nuance":

*"River to the Sea" doesn't have to mean genocide. It could refer
to one democratic state.* They certainly object to the comparisons my peers drew in Poland: *No, you can't compare them to
Nazis, and you can't conflate the swastika with the keffiyeh—it
just represents support for the people of Palestine.*

I don't blame my friends at school. We go to Yale, and
the campus culture is totalizing. Being a Yalie is an identity
unto itself. It's supposed to be transformative. Our professors are supposed to share ideas that will change our lives.
We're here to think hard and to become better people, to
bring our school's motto of "light and truth" into the world,
using the great power and platform that Yale puts into our
hands. Students here love those profound "dining hall conversations" with the supposedly smartest twenty-year-olds
in the country, whose insights we can't enjoy anywhere else.

So how are Jewish Yalies supposed to react when
those dining hall conversations are with students who
want to consign their families to the furnace, or when
their faculty mentors want the same? When they
celebrate and sympathize with Hamas mowing down and
amputating and gang-raping? Denial becomes a reasonable
choice, since facing the truth that they're a Jew before a Yalie—or that the two are at times mutually exclusive—shatters the exclusive, elite identity to which they have committed four years of their Jewish lives and much of their
admiration.

My friends at school are not alone in their struggle.
The world has betrayed its Jews, yet we continue to march
to the beat of foreign drummers. I know Jews who have

converted to Catholicism, forgetting the Inquisition, and Jews who prop up Al Sharpton, forgetting Crown Heights. It should be no surprise that there are Jews who call for an unconditional ceasefire in Gaza, forgetting the hostages, and even Jews who justify October 7 as an act of resistance. Each is living in a totalizing, not-Jewish world which demands that Jews sacrifice and be sacrificed.

Perhaps they admire the foreign worlds for their beautiful art, ideas, and culture. In Poland, we learned of a foreign world that also had beautiful art, ideas, and culture. But this world lacked morality. Majdanek, for instance, was run by a Nazi couple. The wife was an artist. Her husband would assess prisoners who had pleasant complexions, and the Jews he selected would be skinned and their backs gifted to his wife as canvases. In Auschwitz, the Jews in the camp orchestra played classical music as their brothers and sisters marched to their deaths. One young harmonica player saw his aunt in line for the gas chamber and asked her for a hug. She refused, promising to hug him after she was clean from the shower.

Jews in Poland learned in horror that they were Jews first. They responded by *living and dying in dignity*.

Jews today need to remember this, since Jewish history repeats itself over and over. Our Jewish traditions have evolved to bestow us with timeless solutions. Instead of denying the repetition of history embodied by October 7 and its aftermath, we can embrace the wisdom of those who came before us, raising our eyes to a Jewish universe which can *also* offer beautiful art, ideas, and culture, while unconditionally preferring living Jews over dead ones.

No radical change is required for this shift. No Jews need to drop everything today because they have realized that they are Jewish first. They just need to return to the family that loves them. That could mean connecting to Jews throughout time by singing or dancing to Jewish tunes—something we did every day in Poland. It could mean discovering Jewish ethics through Torah, or Jewish faith on Shabbat. Remembering every day that we live by the merit of millions of other Jews, and that we do not forget each other, even when the rest of the world does.

What a difference these small choices make. After October 7, my father began wearing his *yarmulke* again. On the subway, a homeless man saw him and began to speak to him in Hebrew. He asked him for *tzedeka*, or charity, and the two spoke a little Torah. Then he asked my father for a hug, because all this Jew needed in that moment was to feel at home. For this, he knew he could count on the love of a Jewish father.

Our Jewish family isn't perfect. The lessons of the Jewish family aren't easy. We aren't popular. I understand why Jews slip away or even betray us for what appear to be better families—who eventually turn out to be not even friends. But I wish they'd return. We are, after all, a family, and we are in this together.

30

DEI, Antisemitism, and the Future of America

Eyal Yakoby

On Saturday, October 7, like so many college students, I woke up in the late morning after a night out with friends. Still in bed, I checked my phone—and suddenly realized how much my world had diverged from those of my fellow students.

My family group chat was abuzz: "Is Noam safe?" "Everyone stay indoors." "What is happening?" Soon, pictures emerged of charred bodies and hostages being swept away by Hamas in trucks.

I called my father, trying to piece together the disaster that had hit the Jewish homeland. The only words that came to me were "I'm sorry."

As a dual American-Israeli citizen of an age to be an IDF soldier, I could feel only remorse. I should not be at

Eyal Yakoby is a recent graduate of the University of Pennsylvania, where he majored in Political Science and Modern Middle East Studies. Active in the campus fight against radicalism and antisemitism, he has addressed these critical issues before Congress at a House Leadership Press Conference and has testified before the House Judiciary Committee. He has appeared on CNN, ABC, SkyNews, Fox News, and CBS, and has been featured or cited in the *Washington Post*, the *New York Post*, *The Free Press*, Bloomberg, and *Forbes*.

an Ivy League campus, I thought, but instead on my way to liberate Kfar Aza, Kibbutz Be'eri, and the many other towns where Hamas terrorists sought nothing but the murder of Jews.

I got out of bed, wiping away tears. And then the second shock hit: People on my campus and around the world, it was becoming clear, were elated by what had occurred in the Jewish communities surrounding the Gaza Strip. At Penn, faculty and students' social media accounts filled with expressions of perverse joy. A Ph.D. candidate retweeted a picture of the Hamas assault that read, "beautiful sights to wake up to this morning." One student club endorsed a rally the following day, where a speaker said he wanted to salute Hamas for "a job well done."

* * *

By now it is clear that the tidal wave of antisemitism we are seeing on campuses across America and beyond is fueled by a widespread ideology that goes far beyond anything having to do with Jews.

This ideology has many names, but we in America know it best through the phrase "diversity, equity, and inclusion," or DEI. DEI categorizes all social and political actors into binary classes: There are oppressors, and there are the oppressed. Jews, it turns out, are uniformly considered part of the oppressor class, and are therefore immune to prejudice or injustice.

On the other hand, the tactics of pro-Palestinian protesters—demonstrating *en masse*, occupying campus buildings, harassing and assaulting fellow students—not only impede intellectual discourse but do nothing to advance the pursuit of knowledge. Often, these people's behavior crosses the line into intimidation and outright violence. Yet the protesters go unpunished because, in the eyes of DEI bureaucrats, they are the oppressed and therefore have the license to act as they please. One cannot be both oppressor and oppressed, they reason—ultimately exonerating students and faculty for any actions that might otherwise be criticized.

The DEI bureaucracy may have once seemed relatively benign and well-intentioned. But its total lack of accountability in its policies has meant that, instead of being an integral part of the broader community, the DEI bureaucracy operates more like an independent institution, creating a divide rather than fostering inclusivity. Academic freedom and open expression, once the bedrock of universities, have been undermined by DEI in pursuit of its ideological goals.

This has necessarily included a form of antisemitism, positioning Jews as part of the ruling class. It is not new. Many Germans in the first half of the twentieth century claimed that Jews possessed much of Germany's wealth, so they were identified as the source of economic problems, and their elimination was ultimately sought in order to better the lives of the Germans.

On my college campus, this same sick logic emerged after October 7. When I hear while walking to class, "From the River to the Sea, Palestine will be free," it eerily rings the same as "only for Germans."

* * *

While the DEI doctrine has captured the loyalty of a growing number of students, the majority continue to reject it. Most students are not antisemitic, but they are indifferent to the current conflict, which enables bad actors to continue to push the limits of what will go unsanctioned, performing small escalations that in the moment may seem minor but, over time, accumulate into something significant.

In practice, many people today are willing to overlook the actions of those who harass Jewish students, naively believing these individuals won't target the broader society. This notion was starkly challenged when forty Brown University students occupied the President's office, refusing to leave. Nationally, we've seen mass riots against Jewish-owned businesses and widespread vandalism. Failing to address these incidents has directly contributed to the desecration of the Thanksgiving Day Parade and the New York Christmas tree lighting, as well as the burning of American flags.

Because of their binary assumptions of oppressors and oppressed, DEI initiatives often fail to capture the multifaceted nature of identity and conflict. They instead perpetuate a binary worldview that does not allow for the complexity of Jewish identity, which can simultaneously embody aspects of both privilege and persecution. But again, this problem extends far beyond the question of Jews, antisemitism, and

Zionism: It is also a broken lens through which to understand America itself. As a result, our elite institutions have abandoned not only the nuances of American history, but along with them basic conceptions of science, scholarship, truth, and integrity.

If our Founding Fathers could see what has become of our academic institutions, they would be not only disappointed but terrified. In 1790, George Washington told the Hebrew Congregation of Newport, Rhode Island:

> For happily the Government of the United States, which gives to bigotry no sanction, to persecution no assistance, requires only that they who live under its protection should demean themselves as good citizens, in giving it on all occasions their effectual support.

Washington's idea was that, unlike their historical status elsewhere, Jews would not be second-class citizens in the newly formed United States of America. Upon founding this nation, he laid out the ideals of equality and freedom from persecution. In 1819, Thomas Jefferson established the University of Virginia, an institution free from religious indoctrination. Jefferson envisioned a secular education system that would focus on freedom of thought and allow students to be challenged, leading the next generation of Americans.

America's elite institutions have long sought to instill

in the nation's youth these principles of equality and freedom of thought on which all of democracy is based. Jefferson warned of religious doctrine taking over the promotion
of American values of freedom and diversity of thought,
but he never could have imagined the great extent to which
DEI has filled exactly the role of a kind of religious doctrine that he warned about. Schools like the University of
Pennsylvania have become suffused with an ever-expand-
ing set of DEI goals, which now dictate everything from
faculty hiring and promotion to the permissible boundaries
of campus discourse.

***

DEI as such is relatively new. But the perversion of reality
when it comes to Israel, Zionism, and the Jews has been
building in the universities for decades. Einat Wilf, a scholar and former Knesset member, describes what she calls the
"Placard Strategy," according to which Israel (or Zionism,
or the Jews) is equated with any fashionable evil of the day.
The first example of this strategy occurred in 1975 when
the Soviet Union and the Arab world were in cahoots to
pass a United Nations resolution declaring "Zionism is racism." This continued in 2001 during South Africa's Durban
Conference, which somehow, despite images and writings
of Hitler being distributed, is still considered a legitimate
UN-sponsored event. And in 2024, South Africa lambasted the Jewish state, along with a coterie of authoritarian
regimes, bringing suit in the International Court of Justice.

It's honestly a great strategy: Targeting Israel for committing the most heinous crimes, whether it's racism or colonialism or Apartheid or ethnic cleansing or genocide, allows the nations who accuse Israel to deflect attention from their own horrific abuses.

Wilf concludes that the Placard Strategy achieves "its potency by being laundered through UN and international bodies, thereby providing the ultimate stamp of authority to the presentation of the collective Jew as implicated in irredeemable sin."

Her description is identical to what we are seeing at universities. Self-described scholars and university administrators give the same stamp of approval to the social banishment of most Jews (sorry, "Zionists") and the violent disruption of campus life—stopping only when threatened with the loss of funding from either donors or the federal government under Title VI. Academic officeholders grant antisemitism a veneer of legitimacy under the guise of academic contribution. Although these contexts—the UN bodies and elite campuses—may appear distinct, they are intimately interconnected, enabling one to leverage and to draw upon the other in numerous ways.

Recognizing this recurring pattern of legitimization of antisemitism is crucial. It's not merely about responding to present-day expressions of antisemitism, but also understanding its historical disguises and anticipating potential future manifestations. By pulling back these veils and comprehending their underlying prejudices, we empower ourselves to combat antisemitism in its various forms, forging a path toward a fairer and more inclusive society for generations ahead.

* * *

While we consider what role Jews will play in America's future, it is critical to understand the significant overlap between anti-Americanism and antisemitism. It is no coincidence that during the anti-Israel protests, one Penn employee stated that he hopes "America will fall," while another said America "must die," and these tweets were posted in tandem with their anti-Israel, anti-Jewish rhetoric. Moreover, while the flag of the Popular Front for the Liberation of Palestine (PFLP), a designated terrorist organization, was proudly waved at the Penn encampment, four American flags were removed and desecrated just yards away. Professors have infused this ideology into their classrooms, shaping the next generation of Americans to revile the idea not only of a strong Jewish state, but also of a strong United States.

If you capture the hearts and minds of the next generation, you have transcended time. While students remain on campus for only four years, professors are the ones who set the campus culture, teaching students how to think, and what such thinking implies in terms of behavior in society. Rather than teaching virtue, many of our professors teach DEI, while neglecting antisemitism and dismissing Jewish concerns. It is in the best interests of Americans and Jews to expect that our academic institutions prepare the next generation of leaders responsibly, not radicalize students to hate the United States and Jews.

While we in the Diaspora have the privilege of sleeping in late, young people in Israel are being called on to defend their lives and freedoms by force of arms. It is therefore the responsibility of Jews in the Diaspora to take up the fight, not just for our own communities but for society as a whole—and to root out the radicals within our nations.

31

Let Our Existence Disrupt the Narrative

Maia Zelkha

I was nine years old when I visited Israel for the first time. There are three moments that I distinctly remember: seeing the Western Wall, visiting distant relatives in Hebron, and a newspaper article about Batsheva Unterman, who at the time had been recently murdered by a terrorist in the 2008 Jerusalem bulldozer attack. A gruesome photo of her was plastered on the front page. I gathered from the adults around me that she had saved her infant's life moments before she was crushed to death.

I didn't understand much around me—neither the detailed history nor the politics—but I was acutely aware that I was in a place where Jews had lived for thousands of years. We visited ancient Jewish communities, landmarks, and holy cities. Hebrew was both a foreign and familiar language to my ears. I couldn't comprehend any of the chatter around me, but I recognized its sounds and into-

Maia Zelkha is a writer living in Jerusalem. Her work has been featured in publications such as the Jewish Book Council, *Parabola*, *Vision Magazine*, and *Times of Israel* blogs. She is also the founder and editor-in-chief of *Yad Mizrah*, a magazine of contemporary Sephardic and Mizrahi literature, arts, and culture.

nations from knowing the Hebrew alphabet, and from the few prayers and Shabbat songs that I could recite by heart. I knew I was in a place of our peoplehood and history.

That history, I understood from a young age, was frequently marked with hatred and violence. While we walked around Hebron, we entered a small museum dedicated to the 1929 Hebron Massacre, an Arab assault that resulted in the brutal murder of sixty-seven Jews who had been part of Hebron's eight-hundred-year-old Jewish community, with the torture and maiming of hundreds more. A special room was curtained off, with a sign that warned "Caution: Graphic Content." When my parents weren't looking, I entered the mysterious, forbidden space and was confronted with a gallery of black-and-white photos depicting dead children, people wrapped in bloody bandages, and spilled brains. I ran out of the room, unable to catch my breath.

In my child-mind, a simple truth was clear to me: *Those people were murdered because they were Jewish.*

Batsheva Unterman was murdered because she was Jewish.

The people who murdered them hated Jews.

I was a Jew.

When I was a child, my understanding of who I was and how the world related to me was simple, without any modern-day notions or complications of race, nationality, ethnicity, or politics. I didn't understand or care *why* people hated us, or wanted to kill us; just that they did. I didn't understand or care that my mother was Ashkenazi, or that my father was Mizrahi; the color of their skin was of utter, absurd irrelevance. They were Jewish. I was Jewish. We were Jewish.

But as I became older, that initial pureness and simplicity I possessed in understanding who I was became muddled. In university, I was bombarded with strange rhetoric around identity that I found difficult to relate to. Buzzwords like "colonizer," "indigenous," "privileged," "underprivileged," "white," and "BIPOC" fiercely entered all mainstream dialogue on identity, while non-Jews around me pushed me into its various categories. I've been told that I'm "white-passing," I've been told that I look Arab, and I've been told that I look European. I've been told that because my dad is Iraqi and my mom is "white," I am "biracial." I've been told that because I am Jewish I *am* white, and because I am Jewish I am *not* white. The pressure to fit into a certain "box" of American perceptions of race and color made me deeply uncomfortable—I was none of those things. So then, who the hell was I?

* * *

My assertion that I was completely and solely Jewish was rejected by everyone. "That's a religion, not a race." "The idea that Jews are a race is literally what Hitler thought, you're going by his definition?" "It's an ethno-religion, not an actual ethnicity." In many ways, they were right. To be Jewish is not a race or ethnicity. I would even argue that it isn't a religion, since an innumerable number of atheist Jews exist.

If none of those options, then what was "Jewish"? I was deeply confused about how to present my identity to others. I often walked on eggshells when discussing things that were central to my identity, like my connection to Israel, or pride in my nation (which was not America). In my American-Jewish upbringing, I learned about our culture, religion, history, and struggle against persecution. Yet something felt missing in the story. I yearned for a concept that tied it all together.

For a long time I tried to fit into the American narrative of race so others would accept me. I realize now that was only because I lacked the words to fully represent who I was. Much of the fierce dialogue I engaged in at university about my identity as Jew was one that existed only while I was on the defense: things that we weren't, misconceptions about us, the ways people misunderstood our customs, misinformation about Israel. I was desperate to be accepted, to fight and explain why every falsehood people believed about Jews was wrong. I recall that during a conversation with a friend about civil rights, she casually mentioned how I was a white woman who had benefited from my ancestors' whiteness. I stared at her, mouth agape in shock when I reminded her that I'm Jewish. She was unable to recognize the incredible irony of her statement, despite my attempts to explain how Jews historically are not "white."

It was only at the end of my time in university that I ever participated in or led any dialogue at all about all the things that we *were*—our truths and our beliefs. Why did every university speaker's lecture on Jewish history I attended discuss only antisemitism? How come every Jewish student group typically met only to discuss Jew-hatred on campus, and how to combat it? In my last year there, when I presented to the Humanities Institute a research project I wrote on Hebrew poetry, Jewish collective consciousness, and our warrior-poet lineage, my mostly non-Jewish audience was stunned. Many came up to me after and said they had never known about any of those things before. Even more incredibly, many said that they wanted to learn more. I found a fountain of energy, joy, and passion within me when I began telling the narrative of who I truly was as Jew, and not just what I wasn't.

I began to explore that feeling more when I arrived in Israel a few months later, to finish my last semester of university on an exchange program. I experienced a pivotal moment the night before Yom Kippur, when I found myself making my way to the Kotel for the last night of *selichot*, the period of weeks leading up to Rosh Hashana and Yom Kippur when prayers of repentance and forgiveness are chanted. As I made my way through the Old City, I was astonished by the sight of thousands of Jews of all colors, religious levels, and backgrounds literally sprinting with excitement to reach the Western Wall. The entire complex was packed with people, all singing the same songs, standing before the same God, and in the same holy place where our peoplehood was born.

It was then and there that I truly, deeply understood who I was. It was as if I had been shaken with a memory of my pure, simple understanding as a child of what it meant to be a Jew: that we are, at our core, an ancient tribe that survived into the modern era—miraculously I might add, given the numerous attempts to destroy us. That I am part of that tribe, one that for thousands of years has had its own unique land-based rituals, purity customs, oral history, Temple lineage, harvest festivals, history and mythology, spiritual doctrines, tribal symbols, and language. That I come from a lineage of warrior-poets. That we were violently forced from our land into a diaspora for two thousand years, yet always had communities that remained there, despite their struggle to survive routine persecution from invaders. That unlike Spanish, English, French, or Arabic, our language never spread to other parts of the world due to colonialism. And that unlike Christian or Islamic conquests, neither did our spiritual doctrines.

That when Columbus arrived in the Americas, he didn't find Catholic churches, Spanish architecture, communities of Spaniards, or any Spaniards for that matter. Yet when Diaspora Jews throughout history returned to *eretz yisrael*, we returned to a place that had troves of ancient Hebrew manuscripts, artifacts, ruins, Hebrew speakers, active Jewish communities and synagogues, and, most notably, the ruins of our ancient Temple in the direction of which we prayed three times a day.

That even the most isolated, unknown Jewish communities in history, such as the Ethiopian Jews, were found to have maintained highly similar traditions, purity customs, harvest festivals, dietary laws, and Temple memory as their Ashkenazi, Sephardic, and Mizrahi counterparts.

As I stood at the Kotel among thousands of other Jews, I was reminded of what Abraham Joshua Heschel famously wrote in *God in Search of Man*: "Unless being a Jew is of absolute significance, how can we justify the ultimate price which our people was often forced to pay throughout its history?" There was tremendous significance of my individual presence in that moment, absolute significance of each person around me. Simply standing there was enough. I was a tile in a mosaic of the tribe of Israel.

***

It must come as no surprise that only two weeks later, I decided to make Aliyah.

My whole life, I had been told that we need Israel because of how the world rejects us, that we need Israel because in times of historic danger, we have nowhere else to go.

I'm sure there is some truth in that idea, but that's not why I decided to return. I don't need Israel because of the threat of people who hate me. I need Israel because it's the place where my people came from and remained since their conception. Because the thought of being ripped away from it stings my soul. Because it's not only a place where so many of my ancestors lived and died, but because the ones who didn't had constantly yearned for. I need Israel because I refuse to squeeze my identity into words and concepts that it clearly does not fit into—because I refuse to be suffocated by them. I need

Israel because I am part of Israel, because I am a Jew, completely and solely.

It doesn't adhere to the "narrative," to all the words people like to hear these days. Good. Let our existence disrupt the narrative.

Afterword

Zack Bodner

It gives me tremendous pride to see how this book has righted a historic wrong. For thousands of years, the story of the Maccabees was not included in our primary Jewish canon—neither in the Hebrew Bible nor in the Talmud. But today, *Young Zionist Voices* finally offers the beginning of a new Jewish canon, one that proudly highlights the stories of Jews bravely fighting back. Only these are not the Maccabees of the past; these are the Jewish warriors of the future.

Scholars offer differing reasons as to why the two books of Maccabees wound up on the cutting room floor when the Tanach was completed in the second century C.E. But one plausible explanation is that the final curators of the Hebrew Bible, who lived in the wake of the failed Jewish rebellions against the Roman Empire and the destruction of the Second Temple, did not want to validate the use of Jewish force. They were afraid, it seems, that if they showcased Jews standing up to anti-Jewish authoritarianism, it might inspire future generations of Jews to fight back. The Jewish leaders of the time likely believed that the

Zack Bodner is President and CEO of the Oshman Family JCC in Palo Alto, California, which hosts the Z3 Project, which he founded in 2014 as the Zionism 3.0 Conference. He is the author of *Why Do Jewish? A Manifesto for 21ˢᵗ-Century Jewish Peoplehood* (Gefen, 2022).

best way for our people to survive under unfriendly rulers was to keep our heads down and not to rock the boat.

Now with thousands of years of history to prove it, we know this approach doesn't work. Our enemies will come for us no matter how servile we are. It is no coincidence, then, that the founders of Zionism popularized the heroism of the Maccabees by resurrecting their story of Jewish liberation and making it central to the Hanukkah story. It was the early Zionists who flipped the script and highlighted Jewish strength, bravery, and power.

For too long, we have been the "ever-dying people," as the Jewish philosopher Simon Rawidowicz put it. But that old shtetl mindset, which dates all the way back to the second century, was always just a variation of the same slave mentality that has plagued us since the days of Pharoah. Moses knew it had to be abandoned in the desert, left to a time and place when our people didn't know sovereignty, self-governance, and self-protection. When Joshua led the Jews back into our Promised Land, they finally shed their self-doubt. But it returned centuries later with our next dispersion, and it was only with the rise of Zionism and the birth of the modern State of Israel that a new Jew was born once again.

These new Jews—the Israelis—were raised to be strong and resilient. They were trained to stand up and fight, to defend their people not just in Israel but around the world. As in Moses's time, the slave mentality was bred out of these Jews in a single generation by witnessing the world's complacency that allowed six million of their brethren to be slaughtered.

But, despite the success of the Israeli rebirth, there still has existed a version of the shtetl Jew among many in the Diaspora. While not all Diaspora Jews suffer this mind-set, most of us were caught completely unprepared for the terror attacks of October 7, 2023—the worst massacre of Jews in a single day since the Shoah—followed by a tid-al wave of hostility towards all Jews and Zionists around the world.

So, this has now become a new moment for truth for the Jews, and the next generation knows it. As Maya Platek writes in her essay, "The Jewish world stands divided: be-tween those hoping that they'll ride out this wave of an-tisemitism and distancing from Israel, and those who have chosen not to cower and instead to stand tall, even in the face of the world's hatred."

* * *

Fortunately, our new Maccabees know on which side to stand. When so much of the world, especially those carry-ing the banner of progress and the hope for a more ethical world, turned its back on the Jews after October 7, the eyes of our young Zionists were pried open, and the last vestiges of shtetl weakness vanished. Like their Israeli brothers and sisters, young Diaspora Jews were also reborn after Octo-ber 7. They became the ones to stand and be proud. They became the ones to show strength. They became the new Jewish warriors.

As Alissa Bernstein writes here, "Since October 7, many young Jews...understand that to be a Zionist is to fight hate actively, to stand up for our community, to educate our non-Jewish friends, and to shake off those who oppose our very identities."

Still, with the situation so bleak, it may be difficult for some in the establishment to step aside and hand the reins to the new Maccabees. But one of the gifts given to us by these young Zionists is that they not only see the light at the end of the tunnel—they're the ones creating the light. And that's at least one reason to heed the advice of Noah Katz, who writes here, "A good leader knows when it's time to step back and let others do the talking. It is time to let the new generation take the lead."

This is why David Hazony writes in his introduction that these young Zionist voices share "an inner optimism that transcends the fear and pain which has, it seems, engulfed the conversations of older Jews."

Yet, it's more than that. The words of these Zionists overflow with not just optimism, but *hope*—and there is a difference between the two. As Rabbi Jonathan Sacks teaches us, optimism is essentially a passive emotion, while hope is active. It takes little courage to be an optimist, but a great deal of it to have hope. And these young Maccabees are nothing if not courageous. Indeed, through their activism, they are defining the term "Jewish courage" for a new generation. And that should give all of us hope.

Asher Stern says it brilliantly in his essay: Zionism, he writes, "is a journey that embraces the Jewish quality of resilience. Through their resilience, Jews have found the ability to overcome. Zionism is, above all, the expression of the unique Jewish resolve to overcome."

These brave Jewish thought leaders will safeguard the future of our people and show the world how resilient we are. They will shift the narrative from the Jewish people being "ever-dying" to "ever-living." For that is the true meaning of *Am Yisrael Chai.*

Acknowledgments

One of the hardest things I've ever done was to board a plane from Tel Aviv to Boston on October 19, 2023, less than two weeks after the horror of October 7. I was to take part in a three-week, multi-event launch of my previous anthology *Jewish Priorities: Sixty-Five Proposals for the Future of Our People*. Like every Israeli on that plane, I was still in shock. But I was also curious to learn what American Jews were going through.

When I arrived stateside, I was struck by the similarities between the traumas engulfing the two communities—but even more so by the differences.

Israelis, within a week, had responded with overwhelming mobilization, whether military or civilian. We were fighting for our lives, and we all had a role to play. For American Jews, by contrast, the dominant feelings were fear, loneliness, and uncertainty about what to do—feelings that persist, in one form or another, to this day. Young people, especially those on campus, were torn among the instincts to freeze, flee, or fight.

A new book, we hoped, would give young Zionists a voice, showcasing those who understood the need to fight—the new young leaders of the Jewish world. Many of the people I met in the context of *Jewish Priorities* proved invaluable in making *Young Zionist Voices* a reality.

I am deeply grateful to Adam Bellow and David S.

Bernstein, publishers of Wicked Son Books, for helping develop the idea of this book and offering essential guidance throughout the process.

Identifying and reaching out to contributors required no small amount of networking, creativity, and persistence. Most generous of their time and contacts were Blake Flayton, Stuart Halpern, Tatiana Hasson, Michal Hatuel, Eylon Levy, Guy Melamed, Claudia Rubenstein, David Suissa, Maya Sulkin, Bari Weiss, Joel Winton, and Daphna Yizrael.

This volume could never have been produced without the generous support of Michael Steinhardt as well as the Steinhardt Foundation for Jewish Life's President and CEO Rabbi David Gedzelman, through the Z3 Institute for Jewish Priorities. In addition, I received incredible encouragement and much concrete assistance from Rabbi Amitai Fraiman, Director of the Z3 Project, and Zack Bodner, President and CEO of the Oshman Family Jewish Community Center in Palo Alto, California, which hosts the Z3 Project.

To my beloved wife Dikla, I owe gratitude beyond words.

David Hazony
Jerusalem, October 2024

About the Editor

David Hazony is Director and Steinhardt Senior Fellow at the Z3 Institute for Jewish Priorities, and editor of *Jewish Priorities: Sixty-Five Proposals for the Future of Our People* (Wicked Son, 2023).

He is the former editor-in-chief of the journal *Azure* and was the founding editor of TheTower.org. His book *The Ten Commandments: How Our Most Ancient Moral Text Can Renew Modern Life* (Scribner, 2010) was a finalist for the National Jewish Book Award. His translation of Uri Bar-Joseph's *The Angel: The Egyptian Spy Who Saved Israel* (Harper-Collins, 2016) was a winner of the National Jewish Book Award.

He has also edited two earlier anthologies: *Essential Essays on Judaism* by Eliezer Berkovits (Shalem, 2002), and, with Yoram Hazony and Michael B. Oren, *New Essays on Zionism* (Shalem, 2007). He has a Ph.D. in Jewish Philosophy from the Hebrew University and lives in Jerusalem.

Made in the USA
Las Vegas, NV
17 November 2024

12023985R00154